The Rise of Christianity
through the eyes of
Gibbon, Harnack and Rodney Stark

For Christine

The Rise of Christianity
through the eyes of Gibbon, Harnack and Rodney Stark

A Valedictory Lecture
on the occasion of his retirement
from the Chair of Religious Studies,
in the Faculty of Theology and Religious Studies,
delivered in abbreviated form before
the University of Groningen
on 29 January 2010
by

JAN N. BREMMER

Barkhuis
Groningen
2010

Cover image: The martyrdom of St. Alban from a 13th Century manuscript of 'The Life of St. Alban' (Dublin, Trinity College Library, MS E. I. 40, folio 38r); Matthew Paris was both scribe and illuminator for this manuscript. Source image and image description: Wikipedia.
St Alban was martyred at Verulamium on 22 June, but no ancient source states the year. What little is known about Christianity in Roman Britain before Constantine suggests that he was executed under either Decius or Valerian. For reasons unknown, the centre of his cult became Auxerre from which the saint's cult spread in early medieval Gaul and Germany. See T.D. Barnes, *Early Christian Hagiography and Roman History* (Tübingen, 2010) 307-12.

Cover design: Coltsfootmedia, Nynke Tiekstra, Noordwolde
Book design: Barkhuis

ISBN 9789077922705

Second Edition

Contents

Preface

It is a fine custom of the Faculty of Theology and Religious Studies of the University of Groningen to distribute the printed version of inaugural and valedictory lectures immediately after the lecture itself. In my case the interest of the audience was such that the whole print run was exhausted virtually immediately. I am therefore most grateful to Roelf Barkhuis for his generous reaction to the idea of issuing a second edition. For this new version I have corrected a few mistakes, updated the bibliography and added a few sentences.

It is a pleasure to thank Ria Kuipers-Faber for her assistance with the first edition, Frouke Veenstra-Vis, the ideal librarian, for unfailingly procuring books at short notice and Eline Veldt for being such a wonderful student assistant. For helpful comments and useful information I am most grateful to Ken Dowden, Wim Jongman, Wolfram Kinzig, Hans Kippenberg, Birgit van der Lans, Pieter Nanninga, Wilfried Nippel and Mladen Popović. I am indebted to Anders Klostergaard Petersen for allowing me to 'try out' my lecture at Aarhus University in January 2010. Arie Molendijk illuminatingly discussed Harnack and Stark with me. Ton Hilhorst and Yme Kuiper read the whole manuscript as it developed, saved me from many mistakes and improved the argument by their incisive criticisms. Last but not least, Jitse Dijkstra's eagle eye subjected the final manuscript to a thorough scrutiny that made me rethink many a formulation. David Dawson and David Herbert kindly corrected my English and enhanced the overall style.

Jan N. Bremmer
Groningen, 17 April 2010

Mr Rector, ladies and gentlemen,

As the son of a Dutch Calvinist minister, the grandson of a Calvinist minister and the great-grandson of a Calvinist professor of theology, I may perhaps be forgiven for returning to my roots in this valedictory lecture. The last fifty years have seen the spectacular implosion of the Christian Church in the West, and this has led me to look once again at the reasons for its rise in the first three centuries of our era until the victory of Constantine. The spread of Christianity has often been studied, but I would like to concentrate on the explanations adduced from a historical perspective by focusing on the works of three iconic figures, at least in the eyes of not a few, from the last two hundred and fifty years: *The History of the Decline and Fall of the Roman Empire* of Edward Gibbon,[1] the most famous ancient historian of all times, at the end of the eighteenth century; *Die Mission und Ausbreitung des Christentums* of Adolf von Harnack,[2] the greatest historian of early Christianity of all times, around 1900, and *The Rise of Christianity* of Rodney Stark,[3] neither an ancient historian nor a specialist of early Christianity but

---

[1] In text and notes I refer to the authoritative new critical edition: E. Gibbon, *The History of the Decline and Fall of the Roman Empire*, ed. D. Womersley, 3 vols (London, 1995²). For full bibliographies see P.B. Craddock, *Edward Gibbon. A Reference Guide* (Boston, 1987) and, from 1985 to 2003, W. Nippel, 'Literatur zu Gibbon', in E. Gibbon, *Verfall und Untergang des römischen Imperiums*, tr. M. Walter and W. Kumpmann, 6 vols (Frankfurt, 2003) 6.103-14, who also provides an excellent introduction: 'Der Historiker des Römischen Reiches: Edward Gibbon (1737-1794)', *ibidem*, 7-102. I have limited my references to the most recent and informative bibliography and do not annotate well-known facts about the Roman Empire.

[2] I quote from the final edition: A. von Harnack, *Die Mission und Ausbreitung des Christentums in den ersten drei Jahrhunderten* (Leipzig, 1924⁴). In my argument I have happily borrowed formulations from the English translation of the second German edition (1906): A. Harnack, *The Mission and Expansion of Christianity in the First Three Centuries*, tr. J. Moffat, 2 vols (London, 1908), which lacks many of the additions of the later editions and makes therefore easier reading.

[3] R. Stark, *The Rise of Christianity: How the Obscure, Marginal Jesus Movement Became the Dominant Religious Force in the Western World in a Few Centuries* (Princeton, 1996).

perhaps the most provocative sociologist of religion at the end of the twentieth century. We shall try to locate their concerns and explanations within their own times, but we will also take them seriously as scholars by discussing their explanations and approaches. Our investigation does not pretend to present the definitive explanation of the rise of Christianity. Such a major and complicated process cannot be fruitfully reduced to a few simple causes. But if we have succeeded in noticing the ideological presuppositions of the leading scholars, we can perhaps pose better questions and proceed with our investigation on a firmer basis.

1 Edward Gibbon

Edward Gibbon published the first volume of his famous *The History of the Decline and Fall of the Roman Empire* on February 17, 1776, the year of the American independence but also of the appearance of his friend Adam Smith's *An Inquiry into the Nature and Causes of the Wealth of Nations*. Gibbon's book was an immediate success, and its thousand printed copies were sold out in a few weeks, quickly followed by a second edition on 3 June and a third in May 1777. In the following years five more volumes would appear, and Gibbon concluded his work in 1788 with the fall of Constantinople in 1453.

Modern readers will hardly realise that there had not been any such modern narrative history before Gibbon, the sole exception being the slightly earlier *History of England* by the great philosopher and Gibbon's older acquaintance, David Hume.[4] As Arnaldo Momigliano (1908-1987) has argued in a famous article, Gibbon effected a synthesis between the older, antiquarian scholarship and the contemporary grand narratives of the philosophers with their wit and irony;[5] subsequent research has

---

[4] D. Hume, *The History of England, from the invasion of Julius Caesar to the revolution in 1688*, 6 vols (London, 1754-62), cf. J. Pocock, *Barbarism and Religion* (Cambridge, 1999) 2.163-257. For Gibbon and Hume see D. Womersley, *The Transformation of The Decline and Fall of the Roman Empire* (Cambridge, 1989) 20-38; A. Weber, *David Hume und Edward Gibbon: Religionssoziologie in der Aufklärung* (Frankfurt, 1990); S.P. Foster, *Melancholy Duty: the Hume-Gibbon Attack on Christianity* (Dordrecht and Boston, 1997).

[5] Famous article: A.D. Momigliano, *Studies in Historiography* (London, 1966) 1-39 ('Ancient History and the Antiquarian', 1950[1]); see also 40-55 ('Gibbon's Con-

added the classical narrative as another factor that was integrated into this synthesis.[6] Gibbon may thus safely be called the first modern ancient historian.[7]

The *Decline and Fall* is still a delight to read and impresses by its enormous erudition. Gibbon possessed a private library of some 6000 books, which greatly helped the project to develop.[8] One sign of his erudition was his massive employment of the footnote, more than 8350 in this work. Its use on such a scale, a quarter of the about 3200 pages of the whole work, was innovative too in Great Britain, if not, hardly surprisingly, in Germany.[9] Yet few scholars mentioned in the notes will be household names today, and the average modern lay reader will take the work in hand more for a good read because of its wit, irony and eye for scandalous details than for its historical value. The modern ancient historian also soon realises that Gibbon wrote at a time when epigraphy, papyrology, archaeology and source criticism were still *in statu nascendi*, but even scholars will be regularly rewarded by Gibbon's massive reading and shrewd insights.

Undoubtedly, the most striking modern contribution to scholarship on Gibbon is the project of John Pocock who, since he turned seventy-

---

tribution to Historical Method', 1954[1]), cf. M.S. Phillips, 'Reconsiderations on History and Antiquarianism: Arnaldo Momigliano and the Historiography of Eighteenth-Century England', *J. of the History of Ideas* 57 (1996) 297-316; note also W. Ernst, 'Antiquarianismus und Modernität. Eine historiographische Verlustbilanz', in W. Küttler *et al.* (eds), *Geschichtsdiskurs*, 5 vols (Frankfurt, 1993-1999) 2.136-47.

[6] D. Wootton, 'Narrative, Irony, and Faith in Gibbon's *Decline and Fall*', in D. Womersley (ed.), *Edward Gibbon, Bicentenary Essays* (Oxford, 1997) 203-34.

[7] W. Nippel, 'Edward Gibbon und die Anfänge der modernen Althistorie', in G.W. Most (ed.), *Historicization – Historisierung* (Göttingen, 2001) 149-67.

[8] G. Keynes (ed.), *The Library of Edward Gibbon* ([Godalming], 1980[2]); G.W. Bowersock, *From Gibbon to Auden* (Oxford, 2009) 33-42.

[9] G.W. Bowersock, 'The Art of the Footnote', *American Scholar* 53 (1983-1984) 54-62; J. Kaestner, 'Anmerkungen in Büchern. Grundstrukturen und Hauptentwicklungslinien, dargestellt an ausgewählten literarischen und wissenschaftlichen Texten', *Bibliothek – Forschung und Praxis* 8 (1984) 203-26; A. Grafton, *The Footnote* (Oxford, 1997) 97-104; Nippel, 'Der Historiker des Römischen Reiches', 81-89 ('Die Fussnoten als Subtext').

five (!) in 1999, has already published more than 1500 pages in an attempt to find a context for Gibbon's work and life; in other words, to find a place for Gibbon in the Enlightenment.[10] Pocock, then, is one of the most illustrious representatives of the modern trend to contextualise, a development that has hardly been contextualised itself as regards its implications and consequences.[11]

One of Gibbon's great strengths is his style and the crafting of his material. Compliments and criticisms are combined in such a manner that the reader is often left wondering about Gibbon's own opinion.[12] This artful disposition of material is also apparent in his treatment of Christianity. A famous example is a small footnote on Apollonius of Tyana, a neo-Pythagorean religious guru of the later first century AD. Gibbon describes him as follows: 'Apollonius of Tyana was born about the same time as Jesus Christ. His life (that of the former) is related in so fabulous a manner by his disciples, that we are at a loss to discover whether he was a sage, an impostor, or a fanatic' (I.315, note 63).[13] No one can be blind to the suggestion that Jesus and Apollonius are comparable, even though this is not said explicitly. Moreover, the contemporary informed reader could hardly miss the reference to the most outrageous and atheist work of the early Enlightenment, the *Traité des Trois Fameux Imposteurs*, which claimed to expose Moses, Jesus and Muhammad as charlatans,[14] a

---

[10] J. Pocock, *Barbarism and Religion*, 4 vols (Cambridge, 1999-2005). As Pocock (letter of 26 March 2010) informs me, his fifth volume should appear later this year and will deal with the context and reception of Gibbon's fifteenth and sixteenth chapters, although strictly from the point of view of eighteenth-century historiography.

[11] But see P. Burke, 'Context in Context', *Common Knowledge* 8 (2002) 152-77.

[12] Gibbon's style has often been commented upon. See especially P. Craddock, '"Immortal Affectation": Responses to Gibbon's Style', *The Age of Johnson: A Scholarly Journal* 1987, 327-46; Nippel, 'Der Historiker des Römischen Reiches', 89-93 ('Ein spezieller Humor und Stil').

[13] For Apollonius see K. Demoen and D. Praet (eds), *Theios Sophistès. Essays on Flavius Philostratus' Vita Apollonii* (Leiden, 2009).

[14] For Gibbon and Muhammad see B. Lewis, 'Gibbon on Muhammad', in G.W. Bowersock *et al.* (eds), *Edward Gibbon and the Decline and Fall of the Roman Empire* (Cambridge MA and London, 1977) 61-73; Th.-M. Jallais, 'Gibbon et la pierre noire de l'Islam: Quelques remarques sur le chapitre L de *The Decline and*

manuscript copy of which Gibbon owned.[15] The same ambiguous juxtaposition can be observed in a famous sentence from his final chapter, 'In the preceding volumes of this History, I have described the triumph of barbarism and religion' (III.1068), where the reader can hardly fail to infer that religion is not that far removed from barbarism. Indeed, Gibbon's rejection of Christianity is already fully apparent from his first volume, even though he was an unbeliever rather than an atheist;[16] in some ways, he perhaps was, as Peter Brown acutely observes, a theologian *manqué*.[17] His views aroused much contemporary attention and polemics,[18] and he already softened the language of his chapters on Christianity even before the first attacks had been published.[19] As a result, the subsequent volumes were much less controversial, if hardly less sceptical towards Christianity.

Fall of the Roman Empire', in C. d'Haussy (ed.), *Quand religions et confessions se regardent* (Paris, 1998) 167-77; D. Womersley, *Gibbon and the 'Watchmen of the Holy City'* (Oxford, 2002) 147-72.

[15] As is shown by D. Womersley, 'Gibbon's religious characters', in S. Collini *et al.* (eds), *History, Religion, and Culture: British Intellectual History 1750-1950* (Cambridge, 2000) 69-88. For the *Traité* see the edition by S. Berti, *Trattato dei Tre Impostori* (Turin, 1994); more recently, F. Charles-Daubert, *Le 'Traité des trois imposteurs' et 'L'esprit de Spinosa': philosophie clandestine entre 1678 et 1768* (Oxford, 1999); G. Minois, *Le traité des trois imposteurs: histoire d'un livre blasphématoire qui n'existait pas* (Paris, 2009). M. Jacobs, *Strangers Nowhere in the World* (Philadelphia, 2006) 19 notes that the book was printed in The Hague in 1719 but subsequently confiscated by the authorities, which has left us only one printed copy.

[16] For Gibbon's evolving religious views see B.W. Young, "Scepticism in excess': Gibbon and eighteenth-century Christianity', *Historical Journal* 41 (1998) 179-99.

[17] P. Brown, *Society and the Holy in Late Antiquity* (London, 1982) 49-62 ('In Gibbon's Shade') at 52; comparably, D.D. Smith, 'Gibbon in Church', *J. Ecclesiastical History* 35 (1984) 452-63.

[18] See the helpful collection by D. Womersley, *Religious Scepticism. Contemporary Responses to Gibbon* (Bristol, 1997).

[19] M.C. Noonkester, 'Gibbon and the Clergy. Private Vices, Public Virtues', *Harvard Theological Review* 83 (1990) 399-414; Womersley, *Gibbon and the 'Watchmen of the Holy City'*, 13-42.

Gibbon started the first volume of his history with the Antonine period, basically with the Emperor Trajan. The first fourteen chapters relate the gradual decline of the Roman state until the final victory of Constantine in 324 AD. Nowhere is there any mention of Christianity, not even of Constantine's famous vision,[20] until the very last sentence: 'The foundation of Constantinople, and the establishment of the Christian religion, were the immediate and memorable consequences of this revolution' (I.445). The reader who turned the page must therefore have been greatly surprised to find that the last two 'invidious chapters', as Gibbon called them,[21] treated 'The Progress of the Christian Religion, and the Sentiments, Manners, Numbers, and Conditions, of the Primitive Christians' (XV) and 'The Conduct of the Roman Government towards the Christians, from the Reign of Nero to that of Constantine' (XVI). As Gibbon was very interested in his own reputation,[22] it is highly unlikely that this composition was unintentional. He must have realised that in this way the curious reader would look forward with great interest to Gibbon's treatment of the following centuries in which the Christian presence would have to loom large. In a way, these two chapters were a cliffhanger *avant la lettre*, although this effect has been spoiled by the twentieth-century editions of Bury and Womersley, neither of whom lets the two chapters conclude the first volume; in fact, even Pocock postponed the discussion of these chapters in his study of the first volume of the *Decline and Fall* to a later occasion.[23]

Although the two chapters have received several excellent discussions in more recent times, these mainly look at Gibbon's sources or the influence of the Enlightenment.[24] On the other hand, it is my intention to

---

[20] See, most recently, W.V. Harris, 'Constantine's Dream', *Klio* 87 (2005) 488-94; J.N. Bremmer, 'The Vision of Constantine', in A. Lardinois *et al.* (eds), *Land of Dreams* (Leiden, 2006) 57-79.

[21] E. Gibbon, *Miscellaneous Works*, 5 vols (London, 1796-97) 1.153.

[22] This has often been observed, most recently by Womersley, *Gibbon and the 'Watchmen of the Holy City'*.

[23] Pocock, *Barbarism and Religion*, 3.489-500.

[24] See especially Womersley, *The Transformation of* The Decline and Fall, 99-133; Wootton, 'Narrative, Irony, and Faith'; Nippel, 'Der Historiker des Römischen Reiches', 48-63; Pocock, 'Gibbon and the Invention of Gibbon: Chapters 15 and 16 Reconsidered', *History of European Ideas* 35 (2009) 209-16.

take Gibbon seriously as an ancient historian and to ask to what extent his discussion is still helpful and tenable in the light of modern scholarship. This has not been done in recent times,[25] but deserves to be done, given Gibbon's lasting influence on discussions of early Christianity, in particular its rise and the persecutions of the Christians.

Let us start with Chapter XV where Gibbon begins by noticing the scarce material at our disposal regarding 'the first age of the church' (I.446). The scarcity is undoubtedly one of the reasons why he started with the post-apostolic period. More importantly perhaps, in this manner he did not have to pronounce on the historical value of the reports about Jesus and the apostles, although the latter were of course responsible for the first spread of Christianity; even the apostle Paul receives hardly any mention and does not figure in Gibbon's original index.[26] Rather strikingly, Gibbon also strongly distinguished himself from the theologians, who might have described 'Religion as she descended from Heaven, arrayed in her native purity', whereas in his view the historian has the 'melancholy duty' to discover 'the inevitable mixture of error and corruption' here on earth (I.446). With these words Gibbon separated himself from church history as practised until his time and indicated that his would be a secular history.

Having thus rejected a primary, theological, cause for the victory of the Christian faith, Gibbon listed five secondary causes, which he then discussed in order: 1) its inflexibility; 2) its doctrine of a future life; 3) its alleged miraculous powers; 4) its 'pure and austere morals', and 5) its organisation. As the title of Adam Smith's famous book shows, at the end of the eighteenth century scholars became interested not only in 'grand narratives' but also in more social-scientific approaches. Gibbon is a typical representative of the concerns of his own time also in this respect.

It is perhaps not by chance that Gibbon started his list with the inflexibility of the Christians, the *first* cause. If there was one contemporary aspect of religion that he disliked, it was the zeal of believers.[27] That is

---

[25] For a beginning see W.H.C. Frend, 'Edward Gibbon (1737-1794) and Early Christianity', *J. Ecclesiastical History* 45 (1994) 661-72.

[26] Pocock, 'Gibbon and the primitive church', in Collini, *History, Religion, and Culture*, 48-68 at 51 points out that Paul is mentioned only in I.500 (Ch. XV) and I.519 (Ch. XVI); add I.453 (Ch. XV): 'their peculiar apostle'.

[27] Pocock, 'Superstition and Enthusiasm in Gibbon's History of Religion', *Eighteenth*

why he himself never became an atheist, but also why he disliked the attempts at a pagan restoration by Julian the Apostate, a great hero of the Enlightenment.[28] It is also not surprising that he therefore disliked 'the desperate fanaticism of the Jews' (I.454; note also I.516), which he saw as an important cause for the attitude of the Christians. Gibbon's view of the Jews was mainly coloured by the classical sources, especially the horrendous details in Flavius Josephus' description of the civil war in Judaea preceding the fall of Jerusalem in 70 AD and the negative views of Tacitus,[29] who, according to Gibbon (I.456 note 27), was even too positive regarding the Jews, but the often negative attitude of the Enlightenment towards the Jews undoubtedly also played a role.[30]

We may note in passing that Gibbon's negative attitude towards the Jews probably caused the great Jewish classicist Jacob Bernays (1824-1881), the best nineteenth-century specialist on Gibbon,[31] to dislike his discussion of the rise of Christianity.[32] Rather surprisingly, Bernays

---

Century Life 8 (1982) 83-94; L.E. Klein and A.J. La Vopa (eds), *Enthusiasm and Enlightenment in Europe, 1650-1850* (San Marino, CA, 1998).

[28] J.S. Spink, 'The Reputation of Julian the "Apostate" in the Enlightenment', *Studies on Voltaire and the Eighteenth Century* 57 (1967) 1399-1415; R.J. Ziegler, 'Edward Gibbon and Julian the Apostate', *Papers on Language and Literature* 10 (1974) 131-38; G.W. Bowersock, 'Gibbon and Julian', in *Gibbon et Rome à la lumiére de l'historiographie moderne = Université de Lausanne, Publications de la Faculté des Lettres* 22 (1977) 191-217; Womersley, *The Transformation of* The Decline and Fall, 156-68 and *Gibbon and the 'Watchmen of the Holy City'*, 127-43; W. Kinzig, 'Polemics reheated? The Reception of Ancient anti-Christian Writings in the Enlightenment', *Zs. f. Antikes Christentum* 13 (2009) 316-50.

[29] R.S. Bloch, *Antike Vorstellungen vom Judentum. Der Judenexkurs des Tacitus im Rahmen der griechisch-römischen Ethnographie* (Stuttgart, 2002).

[30] A. Hertzberg, *The French Enlightenment and the Jews: The Origins of Modern Anti-Semitism* (New York, 1968); A. Sutcliffe, *Judaism and Enlightenment* (Cambridge, 2003) and 'Judaism and the Politics of Enlightenment', *American Behavioral Scientist* 49 (2006) 702-15.

[31] Having followed Bernays' lectures on Gibbon in Bonn, Ulrich von Wilamowitz-Moellendorff (1848-1931), the greatest classicist of the earlier twentieth century, bought the *Decline and Fall*, which helped to improve his English, cf. his *Erinnerungen: 1848-1914* (Leipzig, 1929²) 87f.

[32] J. Bernays, *Gesammelte Abhandlungen*, ed. H. Usener, 2 vols (Berlin, 1885) 2.206-

greatly preferred the five causes adduced by Voltaire.[33] Yet this is wholly unpersuasive, as mention of some of the reasons Voltaire adduced, such as the wealth of the Christians (whereas in fact the majority of the early Christians were poor: see below) and their systematic dogmatics (which did not develop before the third century), may illustrate. Even though he was frequently identified with him in his own time, Gibbon's historical scholarship far surpassed the often propagandist works of Voltaire.[34]

In his discussion of the inflexibility of the Christians, Gibbon situated emerging Christianity within the world of polytheism, which he characterises really well (I.460-62). He already noted that religion in antiquity was closely interwoven with daily life; in other words, it was 'embedded' in society, as we would say today, to such a degree that there was not yet a word for the concept of religion in the first centuries of Christianity. From the third century onwards we see the development of terms for individual religions, such as Judaism and Christianity,[35] but in its modern meaning the concept of 'religion' would emerge only in Gibbon's own

---

54 ('Edward Gibbons Geschichtswerk') at 224-5; similarly, J. Bernays, *Geschichte der klassischen Philologie. Vorlesungsnachschrift von Robert Münzel*, ed. H. Kurig (Hildesheim, 2008) 135. On Bernays, who refused to become a *Taufjude* to further his career and whose niece Martha had married Freud, see H. Bach, *Jacob Bernays* (Tübingen, 1974); A. Momigliano, *Quinto contributo alla storia degli studi classici e del mondo antico*, 2 vols (Rome, 1975) 1.127-58; J. Glucker and A. Laks (eds), *Jacob Bernays, un philologue juif* (Lille, 1996); J. Bollack, *Ein Mensch zwischen zwei Welten: der Philologe Jacob Bernays* (Göttingen, 2009).

[33] Voltaire, *Histoire de l'établissement du Christianisme* (1777) = *Oeuvres complètes*, ed. L. Moland, vol. 31 (Paris, 1877-1885) 43-116 (= Chapter 13).

[34] P. Turnbull, '"Une marionette infidèle": The fashioning of Edward Gibbon's reputation as the English Voltaire', in Womersley, *Edward Gibbon, Bicentenary Essays*, 279-307.

[35] L. Foschia, 'Le nom du culte et ses dérivés à l'époque impériale', in S. Follet (ed.), *L'Hellénisme d'époque romaine* (Paris, 2004) 15-35; A. ter Brugge, *Between Rome and New Jerusalem* (Diss. Kampen, 2009) 169-87; D. Boyarin, 'Rethinking Jewish Christianity: An Argument for Dismantling a Dubious Category (to which is Appended a Correction of my Border Lines)', *Jewish Quarterly Review* 99 (2009) 7-36 at 12-27; G. Casadio, '*Religio* versus Religion', in J. Dijkstra *et al.* (eds), *Myths, Martyrs, and Modernity: Studies in the History of Religions in Honour of Jan N. Bremmer* (Leiden, 2010) 301-26.

time towards the end of the eighteenth century.[36] To withdraw from religious activities thus meant a withdrawal from all kinds of social events, such as the theatre and festivals, but also from weddings and funerals, as religious rituals were an integral part of the social fabric. And where the Romans would have accepted such behaviour from an old religion like Judaism, it was intolerable for a religion with universal claims.

Gibbon was undoubtedly right that this attitude must have made the Christians unpopular. Much worse, though, will have been the damage done to familial relations. This is already forecast in the New Testament, but reports of the deaths of the martyrs, the so-called *Acta martyrum*, give us several examples of husbands against wives, daughters against fathers, and brothers against sisters.[37] However, not all Christians were inflexible. We must be careful not to be swept along by Gibbon's considerable rhetorical powers. The persecutions, especially the ones in the middle of the third century under the Emperor Decius,[38] show that many Christians immediately dropped their faith under pressure.[39] The

---

[36] Bremmer, '"Religion", "Ritual" and the Opposition "Sacred vs. Profane": Notes towards a Terminological "Genealogy"', in F. Graf (ed.), *Ansichten griechischer Rituale. Festschrift für Walter Burkert* (Stuttgart and Leipzig, 1998) 9-32; E.A. Judge, *The First Christians in the Roman World* (Tübingen, 2008) 404-09 ('Was Christianity a Religion?', 2006[1]).

[37] For this aspect of early Christianity see *Mark* 3.31-35; *Matthew* 12.46-50; *Luke* 8.19-21; K. Bradley, 'Sacrificing the Family: Christian Martyrs and their Kin', *Ancient Narrative* 3 (2003) 150-81; Bremmer, 'The Social and Religious Capital of the Early Christians', *Hephaistos* 24 (2006) 269-78 at 273-4; X. Levieils, *Contra Christianos. La critique sociale et religieuse du christianisme des origins au concile de Nicée (45-325)* (Berlin and New York, 2007) 436-45.

[38] Although J. Rives, 'The Decree of Decius and the Religion of Empire', *J. Roman Studies* 89 (1999) 135-54 argues that Decius did not mean to persecute the Christians, Christian authors certainly believed the contrary, cf. D.G. Martinez, 'The Papyri and Early Christianity', in R. Bagnall (ed.), *The Oxford Handbook of Papyrology* (Oxford, 2009) 590-622 at 605-06 with arguments in their favour.

[39] R. Lane Fox, *Pagans and Christians* (London, 1986) 456-7; W. Kinzig and M. Wallraff, 'Das Christentum des 3. Jahrhunderts zwischen Anspruch und Wirklichkeit', in D. Zeller (ed.), *Christentum I* (Stuttgart, 2002) 331-88 at 361-64; W. Ameling, 'The Christian *lapsi* in Smyrna, 250 A.D. (*Martyrium Pionii* 12-14)', *Vigiliae Christianae* 62 (2008) 133-60.

very moment that Christianity started to make major inroads into the Roman population, there must have been plenty of less convinced and more flexible followers of Christ.[40] Yet there evidently remained a group of hard core Christians who were prepared to die for their faith and thus will have inspired others to persevere.

Gibbon's *second* cause is the Christian idea of the immortal soul (I.463-71). Rather perceptively, he noted that the Greeks and Romans did not really invest in a belief in the afterlife,[41] unlike the Druids, Indians and Egyptians (I.464-5). Moreover, he also noted that 'the mysterious dispensations of Providence' had affected the absence of belief in the immortality of the soul in the Old Testament. According to him, it was the Pharisees that started to accept the idea of the immortal soul as well as the existence of a heaven and a hell, which subsequently was embraced 'with the zeal which has always formed the characteristic of the nation' (I.466). Like Hume and many other English contemporaries,[42] Gibbon was sceptical about both the existence of 'everlasting felicity' and the immortality of the soul, which had come under fierce philosophical attack in the eighteenth century.[43] Yet it was not the belief in the immortal soul,[44] which anyway emerged fairly late in Christianity,[45] nor the belief in a kind of heaven and hell, which we already find among the

---

[40] K. Hopkins, *A World full of Gods: Pagans, Jews, and Christians in the Roman Empire* (London, 1999) 93f.

[41] Bremmer, *The Rise and Fall of the Afterlife* (London and New York, 2002) 7f.

[42] K. Thomas, *The Ends of Life* (Oxford, 2009) 226-35.

[43] 'Everlasting felicity': Foster, *Melancholy Duty*, 129-61. Soul: A. Thomson, *Bodies of Thought. Science, Religion, and the Soul in the Early Enlightenment* (Oxford, 2008).

[44] Rightly rejected by R. MacMullen, *Changes in the Roman Empire* (Princeton, 1990) 136; note also the objections of P. Veyne, *Quand notre monde est devenu chrétien (312-394)* (Paris, 2007) 49-52.

[45] M. Van Uytfanghe, 'Platonisme et eschatologie chrétienne. Leur symbiose graduelle dans les Passions et les panégyriques des martyrs et dans les biographies spirituelles (IIe - VIe s.)', in A.A.R. Bastiaensen *et al.* (eds), *Fructus Centesimus. Mélanges G.J.M. Bartelink* (Steenbrugge and Dordrecht, 1989) 343-62 and 'Platonisme II', in L. Holtz and J.-C. Fredouille (eds), *De Tertullien aux Mozarabes. Mélanges Jacques Fontaine*, 3 vols (Paris, 1992) 1.69-95.

Orphics,[46] but the resurrection that made the greatest impact on the pagan world, as has only recently become clear.[47] Already from Neronian times onwards, the motifs of apparent death and resurrection can be found in ancient novels.[48] In the second century, pagan magicians started being credited with the power to resurrect,[49] and at least one cult seems to have associated its god with a resurrection.[50] The third-century biography of the pagan 'saint' Apollonius of Tyana contains a detailed description of the resurrection of a girl,[51] and in the same century even the god Attis became credited with a resurrection.[52]

Also Gibbon's *third* cause, the attraction through miracles (I.471-75), is influenced by contemporary discussions. This becomes immediately clear at the beginning of his argument, where he speaks about 'the occa-

---

[46] A. Bernabé, 'Imagen Órfica del Más Allá', in A. Bernabé and F. Casadesús (eds), *Orfeo y la tradición órfica*, 2 vols (Madrid, 2009) 1.623-56.

[47] On the resurrection see K. Schneider, *Studien zur Entfaltung der altkirchlichen Theologie der Auferstehung* (Bonn, 1999); Bremmer, *Rise and Fall of the Afterlife*, 41-55; B. Feichtinger, 'Quid est autem homo aliud quam caro...? (Tert. Adv. Marc. 1.24). Aspekte spätantiker Körperlichkeit', *Jahrbuch für Antike und Christentum* (2007 [2009]) 5-33; D.Ø. Endsjø, *Greek Resurrection Beliefs and the Success of Christianity* (New York, 2009).

[48] The pioneering study is G. Bowersock, *Fiction into History: Nero to Julian* (Berkeley, Los Angeles, London, 1994) 99-119; add R. Kany, 'Der Lukanische Bericht von Tod und Auferstehung Jesu aus der Sicht eines hellenistischen Romanlesers', *Novum Testamentum* 28 (1986) 75-90; V. Schmidt, 'Lukian über die Auferstehung der Toten', *Vigiliae Christianae* 49 (1995) 388-92.

[49] Polemo, *De physiognomia*, pp.160-4 Förster; Lucian, *Lover of Lies* 13 and *Alexander of Abounoteichos* 24; Apuleius, *Met.* 2.28; *Papyri Graecae Magicae* XIII.279-82.

[50] Tertullian, *De praescriptione haereticorum* 40.

[51] Philostratus, *Life of Apollonius* 4.45, cf. Bowersock, *Fiction as History*, 109-10; D. Praet, 'Pythagoreanism and the Planetary Deities: the Philosophical and Literary Master-Structure of the *Vita Apollonii*', in Demoen and Praet, *Theios Sophistes*, 283-320 at 292 and 295; note also the often overlooked mention in *Historia Augusta*, Vita Aureliani 24.8.

[52] Hippolytus, *Ref.* 5.8.22-24 (and 5.9.8); Firmicus Maternus, *De errore profanarum religionum* 3.1, cf. Ph. Borgeaud, *La mère des dieux: de Cybèle à la vierge Marie* (Paris, 1996) 79-88, 146-53, 155.

sional prodigies, which might sometimes be effected by the immediate interposition of the Deity when he suspended the laws of Nature for the service of religion' (I.471). These words are clearly inspired by Hume's famous definition of the miracle: 'a transgression of a law of nature by a particular volition of the Deity, or by the interposition of some invisible agent'.[53] Miracles were one of the battlegrounds between believers and unbelievers in the eighteenth century,[54] and Gibbon joined the debate with gusto. Thus he wickedly remarks that 'the knowledge of foreign languages was frequently communicated to the contemporaries of Irenaeus, though Irenaeus himself was left to struggle with the difficulties of a barbarous dialect whilst he preached the gospel to the natives of Gaul'.[55] And he mischievously notes that in the days of Irenaeus, 'the resurrection of the dead was very far from being esteemed an uncommon event' and that 'the persons thus restored to their prayers had lived afterwards among them many years' (I.472-3), although the latter detail is not in Irenaeus.[56]

In his studies on the Christianisation of the Roman Empire, Ramsay MacMullen still attaches much value to Gibbon's argument.[57] And

---

[53] I quote from the edition in D. Hume, *Dialogues Concerning Natural Religion*, ed. R.H. Popkin (Indianapolis and Cambridge, 1998^2 [1748^1]) 112 n. 4. For the influence of Hume's treatise on Gibbon see Foster, *Melancholy Duty*, 93-127.

[54] See most recently R.M. Burns, *The Great Debate on Miracles: From Joseph Glanvill to David Hume* (Lewisburg, PA, 1981); D. Wootton, 'Hume's "Of Miracles": Probability and Irreligion', in M.A. Stewart (ed.), *The Philosophy of the Scottish Enlightenment* (Oxford, 1990) 191-229; several studies by P. Harrison: 'Newtonian Science, Miracles, and the Laws of Nature', *J. History of Ideas* 56 (1995) 531-53; 'Prophecy, Early-Modern Apologetics, and Hume's Argument against *Miracles*', *ibidem* 60 (1999) 241-57 and 'Miracles, Early Modern Science, and Rational Religion', *Church History* 75 (2006) 493-511.

[55] I.472, cf. Irenaeus, *Adversus haereses*, *Praefatio* 3 Rousseau/Doutreleau.

[56] Cf. Irenaeus, *Adversus haereses* 2.31.2 Rousseau/Doutreleau (Gibbon refers to 2.56.2 Grabe): *reversus est spiritus mortui et donatus est homo orationibus sanctorum.*

[57] R. MacMullen, *Paganism in the Roman Empire* (New Haven and London, 1981) 96; *Christianizing the Roman Empire* (New Haven and London, 1984) 25-29 and *Changes in the Roman Empire*, 140-1; similarly, W. Reinbold, *Propaganda und Mission im ältesten Christentum* (Göttingen, 2000) 317-22.

indeed, there can be no doubt that miracles figure prominently in the Christian tradition of the first centuries. The Gospels are full of Jesus' miracles; *Acts* mentions miracles as causes of conversion, and the *Apocryphal Acts of the Apostles*, which can be dated from about 150-220 AD, teem with them. The nature of these miracles is well summarized by *Matthew* (10.8): 'Cure the sick, raise the dead, cleanse the lepers, cast out demons' (tr. NRSV). In *Acts*, these miracles are sometimes followed by the conversion of a whole town (9.32-35), just as they are in the *Apocryphal Acts of John* (42). The problem with most of these descriptions, though, is that either the miracles themselves, such as a resurrection, or their effects, such as conversions of whole towns, are highly improbable.[58]

Moreover, within Christianity itself, belief in miracles already started to become problematic in the later second century.[59] Evidently, we have to do with a kind of missionary discourse that should not be confused with reality, although their popularity suggests that there was a large market for such stories. This is of course not surprising in a world that hardly knew proper medical care. Surely, just like today, miracles must have often been seen as the only possibility in desperate situations. The Christians had realised this niche in the religious market and exploited it as no other contemporary religious cult. Reports of miracles may well have produced converts, but our evidence for that result is extremely slim.[60]

Having disposed of the Christian miracle, Gibbon turned to his *fourth* cause, the virtues of Christianity (I.475-82), concentrating on two reasons for conversion in particular. First, he mentioned the possibility

[58] M. Frenschkowski, 'Religion auf dem Markt', in M. Hutter *et al.* (eds), *Hairesis. Festschrift für Karl Hoheisel = Jahrbuch für Antike und Christentum, Erg.* 34 (Münster, 2002) 140-58.

[59] Harnack, *Mission und Ausbreitung*, 225-26, 234; M. van Uytfanghe, 'La controverse biblique et patristique autour du miracle, et ses répercussions sur l'hagiographie dans l'Antiquité tardive et le haut Moyen Âge latin', in E. Patlagean *et al.* (eds), *Hagiographie, Cultures et Sociétés, IVe–XIIe siècles* (Paris, 1981) 205-33; J. den Boeft, 'Miracles Recalling the Apostolic Age', in A. Hilhorst (ed.), *The Apostolic Age in Patristic Thought* (Leiden, 2004) 51-62.

[60] See also the excellent discussion of D. Praet, *De God der goden. De christianisering van het Romeinse Rijk* (Kapellen en Kampen, 1995) 62-69.

of criminals receiving remission of sins (I.476). Undoubtedly, this was a feature of early Christianity,[61] but there is no indication that it led to many converts: Gibbon provides not a single example, which he certainly would have done if he had found one. A second cause was the very strict and world-abstaining morality of the Church: the opposition to luxury, the stress on chastity and marriage, and the 'criminal disregard of public welfare' (I.482). Although there can be little doubt that these factors will have played a role, it is also clear that Gibbon's observations lack every nuance. Early Christianity was not a homogeneous sect, but a movement with great differences in opinion and practices amongst believers as well as with many local variations.[62] Even though there were strong family resemblances between congregations,[63] they were far from identical. True, after the first century most Christians were poor,[64] but, then, most people of the Roman Empire were poor. Yet there were also well-to-do and wealthy women and men in the first centuries who had become followers of Christ: the theme of wealth already plays a major role in the *Shepherd* of Hermas, an early second-century and very popular Christian treatise from Rome,[65] and is still heavily discussed in the writings of Clement of Alexandria (ca. 150-215) and Tertullian of Carthage (ca. 160-220).[66] Moreover, the latter (*Apol.* 42.1-3) frequently

[61] E. Dassmann, *Sündenvergebung durch Taufe, Busse und Martyrerfürbitte in den Zeugnissen frühchristlicher Frömmigkeit und Kunst* (Münster, 1973); A.D. Fitzgerald, 'Penance', in S.A. Harvey and D.G. Hunter (eds), *The Oxford Handbook of Early Christian Studies* (Oxford, 2008) 786-807.

[62] C. Auffarth, 'Die frühen Christentümer als lokale Religion', *Zs. f. Antikes Christentum* 7 (2003) 14-26.

[63] For the term see C. Ginzburg, 'Family Resemblances and Family Trees: Two Cognitive Metaphors', *Critical Inquiry* 30 (2004) 537-56.

[64] G. Schöllgen, *Ecclesia sordida? Zur Frage der sozialen Schichtung frühchristlicher Gemeinden am Beispiel Karthagos zur Zeit Tertullians* (Münster, 1984). This can now also be illustrated by the early Christian diet, cf. the fascinating study of L.V. Rutgers *et al.*, 'Stable isotope data from the early Christian catacombs of ancient Rome: new insights into the dietary habits of Rome's early Christians', *J. Archaeological Science* 36 (2009) 1127-34.

[65] For its popularity see Martinez, 'Papyri and Early Christianity', 600; R.S. Bagnall, *Early Christian Books in Egypt* (Princeton and London, 2009) 40-49.

[66] D. Groh, 'Upper-Class Christians in Tertullian's Africa. Some Observations',

stresses that Christians did not isolate themselves from the pagan world but were fully part of it. How else would they have survived?[67]

On the other hand, Gibbon is clearly right that chastity played a prominent role in early Christianity; this aspect has often been discussed in recent times and need not detain us here.[68] However, Gibbon's interest in sex has received much less attention than many other aspects of his work.[69] He clearly loved to read about it in the ancient historians, even though he had to concede that it sometimes was 'not easy to translate their faithful description into the decency of modern language' (I.116). That is why he always printed the more saucy details in either Greek or Latin, as for example in his description of the wife of the Emperor Justinian, Theodora, who apparently had been a consummate sexual entertainer (II.565). Here too his sense of irony and wit did not leave him. About the Emperor Gordian II (238 AD) he observed: 'Twenty-two acknowledged concubines, and a library of sixty-two thousand volumes, attested the variety of his inclinations; and from the productions which he left behind him, it appears that the former as well as the latter were designed for use rather than for ostentation' (I.195). And about Origen (ca. 185-254), who seems to have castrated himself by following Jesus' words that there are those 'who have made themselves eunuchs for the sake of the kingdom of heaven' (*Matthew* 19.12), Gibbon notes: 'As it was his general practice to allegorize scripture, it seems unfortunate that, in this instance only, he should have adopted the literal sense' (I.480 note

Studia Patristica 16 (1985) 41-47; J. Ulrich, 'Clemens Alexandrinus' "Quis dives salvetur" als Paradigma für die Beurteilung von *Reichtum* und Geld in der Alten Kirche', in M. Welker and M. Wolter (eds), *Gott und Geld* (Neukirchen-Vluyn, 2007) 213-38; S.R. Holman (ed.), *Wealth and Poverty in Early Church and Society* (Grand Rapids, 2008).

[67] For a balanced discussion see G. Schöllgen, 'Integration und Abgrenzung: die Christen in der städtischen Gesellschaft', in Zeller, *Christentum I*, 302-400.

[68] For good surveys see P.F. Beatrice, 'Keuschheit', in *Theologische Realenzyklopädie* 18 (1989) 120-30; P. Brown, *The Body and Society: men, women, and sexual renunciation in early Christianity: twentieth anniversary edition with a new introduction* (New York, 2008) xxi-lxvii.

[69] But see B. Young, 'Gibbon and sex', *Textual Practice* 11 (1997) 517-37; Nippel, 'Der Historiker des Römischen Reiches', 89-92.

96).[70] In the end, we should not forget that Gibbon also was a contemporary of the infamous Marquis de Sade.

Finally, unlike what Gibbon suggests, it simply is not true that the Christians refused to defend the Empire. We have several notices about military martyrs, not all untrustworthy,[71] and Tertullian (*Apol.* 42) explicitly denies the accusation. In fact, the Christian tradition has been often wavering between absolute pacifism and the glorification of war for God and country. The Scottish sociologist of religion Steve Bruce has illuminatingly compared religions to seas from which one can catch different fishes. Yet not all seas, as he notes, support the same species.[72] Unlike Islam, for example, early Christianity contained a pacifist element from its very beginning, just like Buddhism..[73]

Gibbon's *fifth* and final cause is the quality of the early Christian 'government of the church' (I.482-513).[74] Having wrongly observed that 'the primitive Christians were dead to the business and pleasures of the

---

[70] We should not confuse Origen's interpretation with the literalism of modern fundamentalism, which is a fairly recent phenomenon, cf. P. Burke, 'The Rise of Literal-Mindedness', *Common Knowledge* 2 (1993) 108-21.

[71] H. Delehaye, *Les légendes grecques des saints militaires* (Paris, 1909); A.J. Visser, 'Christianus sum, non possum militare: soldatenmartyria uit de derde eeuw', *Ned. Archief v. Kerkgeschiedenis* 48 (1967-8) 5-19; G.E.M. de Ste. Croix, *Christian Persecution, Martyrdom, and Orthodoxy* (Oxford, 2006) 169-73; David Woods' website 'The Military Martyrs' (http://www.ucc.ie/milmart/#Top).

[72] S. Bruce, *Fundamentalism* (Cambridge and Malden, 2008^2) 103f.

[73] For early Christianity see J. Roldanus, 'De vroege kerk en de militaire dienst', *Kerk en Theologie* 33 (1982) 182-202; P.W. van der Horst, *De onbekende God* (Utrecht, 1988) 210-28; H.C. Brennecke, '»An fidelis ad militiam converti possit«? [Tertullian, de idololatria 19,1]. Frühchristliches Bekenntnis und Militär im Widerspruch?', in U. Heil *et al.* (eds), *Die Weltlichkeit des Glaubens in der Alten Kirche, Festschrift für Ulrich Wickert zum siebzigsten Geburtstag* (Berlin and New York, 1997) 179-232; H.L. Barth, 'Das Verhältnis des frühen Christentums zum Militär', in W. Blümer *et al.* (eds), *Alvarium. Festschrift Christian Gnilka = Jahrbuch für Antike und Christentum, Erg.* 33 (Münster, 2002) 1-25; K.L. Noethlichs, 'Krieg III', in *Reallexikon für Antike und Christentum* (= *RAC*) 22 (2008) 52-67.

[74] For this cause and the others of Gibbon see also D. Kyrtatas, 'The Significance of Leadership and Organisation in the Spread of Christianity', in W.V. Harris (ed.), *The Spread of Christianity in the First Four Centuries* (Leiden, 2005) 53-68.

world' (I.482) and misleadingly noted that the Christian societies 'were united only by the ties of faith and charity' (I.484: see below), he continued with a discussion of the presbyters and bishops, the two pillars of the Christian congregations, if mainly concentrating on the latter. Gibbon rightly points to the pre-eminence of the bishops of the major cities, such as Rome, Carthage and Ephesus. They were the ones who had to look after the money of the Church, and charity undoubtedly was an important factor in the growth of Christianity,[75] as Gibbon rightly notes, although he cannot refrain from also commenting that by some of the bishops the riches of the Church 'were perverted to the purposes of private gain, of fraudulent purchases, and of rapacious usury' (I.493), reproaches that sound all too familiar at this very moment in time. On the other hand, it becomes less clear from Gibbon's analysis that the rise of the bishop was closely connected to the rise of Christianity. It was only in the first half of the third century, with Cyprian of Carthage in the West and other bishops in the East, that salaried, ordained and lifelong bishops started to appear.[76] Originally, the Greek term for bishop, *episkopos*, meant 'overseer' in the Athenian Empire,[77] and it seems to have been one of several terms the early Church derived from the Athenian democracy, such as also *ekklêsia* and *leitourgia*.[78] Although, initially, it was often used

---

[75] Reinbold, *Propaganda und Mission*, 323-26; P. Brown, *Poverty and Leadership in the Later Roman Empire* (Hanover NH, 2002) 16-26; Bremmer, 'Social and Religious Capital of the Early Christians', 270-71; see also § 2.

[76] E. Dassmann, *Ämter und Dienste in den frühchristlichen Gemeinden* (Bonn, 1994) 49-73 (hardly persuasive); C. Methuen, 'Widows, bishops and the struggle for authority in the Didascalia apostolorum', *J. Ecclesiastical History* 46 (1995) 197-213; G. Schöllgen, *Die Anfänge der Professionalisierung des Klerus und das kirchliche Amt in der Syrischen Didaskalie = Jahrbuch für Antike und Christentum, Erg.* 26 (Münster, 1998) and 'From Monepiscopate to Monarchical Episcopate: The Emergence of a New Relationship between Bishop and Community in the Third Century', *The Jurist* 66 (2006) 111-28.

[77] F. Kirbihler, 'L. Cusinius, épiscopos (sic) à Ephèse', *Jahreshefte des Österreichischen Archäologischen Institutes in Wien* 74 (2005) 151-73 at 155-59. Highly interestingly, *episkopos* has now also appeared in a Sanskrit text, cf. H. Falk, 'Greek Style Dedications to an Indian God in Gandhara', *Indo-Asiatische Zeitschrift* 13 (2009) 25-42 at 29-31 (with thanks to Hans Bakker).

[78] A. Hilhorst, 'Termes chrétiens issus du vocabulaire de la démocratie Athénienne',

in the plural for members of the Christian clergy, *episkopos* gradually developed into the meaning 'bishop'.[79] At the same time, we can observe the rise of the terms 'clergy' and 'laity', additional indications of the professionalisation of the bishops and their staffs as well as of the growing distance between them and the rest of the Church.[80] Charity (above), cemeteries,[81] and the catechesis for the newly converted now required full time attention from persons without other offices or occupations.

Gibbon also noted very perceptively that the Christian hierarchy was one of its great strengths, whereas pagan priesthoods were just honorary local offices that were not connected to priesthoods elsewhere in the Empire; moreover, we may add, these often lasted only for a limited period of time and could even be held by adolescents.[82] In the final struggle between pagans and Christians, pagan priests were no match for the Christian bishops (I.497-8). These observations on the bishops perhaps reflect Gibbon's own attitude towards the Church as an established institution. Although no believer, Gibbon supported 'our Dear Mamma the Church of England' as one of the pillars of the establishment because he was opposed to political radicals and religious fanatics. In the end, *Staatsraison* was more important for him than his own religious conviction.[83]

Filología Neotestamentaria 1 (1988) 27-34; E.A. Judge, 'Kultgemeinde', in *RAC* 22 (2008) 393-438 at 402-5; K.L. Noethlichs, 'Liturgie I', in *RAC* 23 (2008) 208-30.

[79] H. Solin, '*Episcopus* und Verwandtes. Lexikographisches und Namenkundliches aus der christlichen Frühzeit Roms', *Philologus* 150 (2006) 232-50; C. Rico, '"Episcopoi" (sic), "presbyteroi" et "diakonoi" dans la Bible et la littérature chrétienne des deux premiers siècles', *Revue Biblique* 115 (2008) 127-34.

[80] A. Faivre, 'Kleros', in *RAC* 21 (2006) 65-96 and 'Laie', in *RAC* 22 (2008) 826-53.

[81] For early Christian burials see E. Rebillard, *Religion et sépulture. L'Église, les vivants et les morts dans l'Antiquité tardive* (Paris, 2003); A.M. Yasin, 'Funerary Monuments and Collective Identity: From Roman Family to Christian Community', *Art Bulletin* 87 (2005) 433-57.

[82] J.B. Connelly, *Portrait of a Priestess* (Princeton and London, 2007); B. Dignas and K. Trampedach (eds), *Practitioners of the Divine in Ancient Greece* (Cambridge MA, 2008).

[83] 'Dear Mamma': J.E. Norton, *The Letters of Edward Gibbon*, 3 vols (London, 1956) 1.305, cf. W. Nippel, 'Edward Gibbon, das antike Christentum und die anglikanische Kirche', in S. Ehrenpreis *et al.* (eds), *Wege der Neuzeit. Festschrift Heinz Schilling* (Berlin, 2007) 241-67.

Gibbon concluded the chapter with a subtle *gran finale*. Having first noted that none of the miracles by Jesus or his disciples was mentioned by Greek or Roman sages, he proceeded to observe that they did not refer either to 'the praeternatural darkness' of three hours that followed the death of Christ (*Luke* 23.44-45), although both Seneca and Pliny the Elder were much interested in unusual eclipses. The latter, however, limited himself to 'the singular defect of light which followed the murder of Caesar, when, during the greatest part of a year, the orb of the sun appeared pale and without splendour', a phenomenon probably caused by a catastrophic eruption of Mt Etna.[84] That is all Gibbon says (I.512-13), although of course knowing that the darkness had been adduced by contemporary Christians as a miracle that graced Jesus' death at the cross.[85] Because Gibbon's remarks come at the end of his chapter, the intelligent reader is left in no doubt about the implication of this observation: no mention, no darkness. But if there was no darkness, the same reader must have wondered, what about the reality of the Passion or the resurrection?

After his discussion of the five causes, Gibbon dedicated the final chapter (XVI) of his first volume to the persecutions (I.514-81). Although highly readable and still stimulating, this discussion is not always relevant to my theme of the rise of Christianity. That is why I shall limit myself to one aspect, the number of martyrs, and will come back to the influence of martyrdom in the last section (§ 3). Somewhat simplifying we can say that the less sympathetic a historian is to Christianity, the lower the number of martyrs will be. Gibbon is no exception. His main argument for the 'inconsiderable number of martyrs' (I.540-1) is the statement by Origen (*Contra Celsum* 3.8) that the number of martyrs was rather low. This is true, but Origen wrote in 248 AD, just before the Emperor Decius (249-251) initiated the first empire-wide persecution.[86] And although Gibbon rightly notices that Bishop Dionysius of Alexandria enumerates only seventeen Alexandrian martyrs by name, he neglects to mention

[84] J.T. Ramsey and A. Lewis Licht, *The Comet of 44 B.C. and Caesar's Funeral Games* (Atlanta, 1997) 99-107.

[85] Womersley, *The Transformation of* The Decline and Fall, 124-25. Gibbon seems to have written an 'ample dissertation' on this darkness, which has not been preserved, cf. Womersley, *Gibbon and the 'Watchmen of the Holy City'*, 340f.

[86] On the passage see also Harnack, *Mission und Ausbreitung*, 505 n. 1.

that Eusebius, our source, continues by quoting Dionysius that 'many others throughout the (Egyptian) cities and villages were torn in pieces by the pagans' and that many others had died when wandering in deserts and mountains in order to escape the persecutions.[87]

The same sloppiness regarding the sources appears in his discussion of the treatment and number of the martyrs during the 'Great Persecution' of Diocletian.[88] To prove that arrested Christians were not that badly treated, he adduces a passage from Eusebius' *Martyrs of Palestine* (12) that the Christians could build chapels and freely practise their religion in the copper mines of Palestine (I.577). Now besides the fact that such hard labour was hardly fun,[89] it is mentioned in Eusebius' next chapter that as soon as the authorities had noticed this behaviour, they scattered the Christians to Cyprus, Lebanon and other parts of Palestine; moreover, the four leaders were put on trial and burnt to death when they refused to deny their faith. Equally unsatisfactory is Gibbon's suggestion that some Christians voluntarily gave themselves up to the Roman magistrates to alleviate their debts, to expiate their sins or to profit from the Christian charity bestowed on prisoners (I.577-8), as none of these suggestions is supported by any evidence. Voluntary martyrdom has recently attracted much attention,[90] but is not that easy to explain,

---

[87] Eusebius, *Hist. Eccl.* 6.41-42.

[88] For this persecution see especially W.A. Löhr, 'Some Observations on Karl-Heinz Schwarte's "Diokletian's Christengesetz"', *Vigiliae Christianae* 56 (2002) 75-95; De Ste. Croix, *Christian Persecution*, 35-78 (with very useful additions by J. Streeter).

[89] F. Millar, *Government, Society, and Culture in the Roman Empire* (Chapel Hill and London, 2004) 120-50 ('Condemnation to Hard Labour in the Roman Empire, from the Julio-Claudians to Constantine').

[90] C. Butterweck, *"Martyriumssucht" in der Alten Kirche? Studien zur Darstellung und Deutung frühchristlicher Martyrien* (Tübingen, 1995); J.-L. Voisin, 'Prosopographie des morts volontaires chrétiens (en particulier chez Eusèbe de Césarée)', in M.-F. Baslez and F. Prévot (eds), *Prosopographie et histoire religieuse* (Paris, 2005) 351-62; A.R. Birley, 'Voluntary Martyrs in the Early Church: Heroes or Heretics?', *Cristianesimo nella Storia* 27 (2006) 99-127; A. Dearn, 'Voluntary Martyrdom and the Donatist Schism', *Studia Patristica* 39 (2006) 27-32; De Ste. Croix, *Christian Persecution*, 153-200 (the chapter was composed in the 1950s, but never published; the notes have been well updated).

as we are rarely able to get a close look at the motives of these martyrs. Yet modern analogies from the Near East and South Asia suggest that people who are prepared to die for their faith or ideology are far less uncommon than we perhaps would like to believe.

Gibbon quotes Eusebius as stating that there had been only 92 martyrs in Palestine. As Palestine, according to Gibbon, constituted the sixteenth part of the Eastern Empire, 'the whole might consequently amount to about fifteen hundred, a number which, if it is equally divided between the ten [actually: eight] years of the persecution, will allow an annual consumption of one hundred and fifty martyrs'. Applying the same reasoning to other parts of the Roman Empire, Gibbon eventually reached the number of 'somewhat less than two thousand persons' (I.579). Yet once again he makes Eusebius say things he did not say, as he only enumerated the martyrs he personally knew.[91] Moreover, Eusebius stressed the *myrioi*, 'tens of thousands', of martyrs of the Diocletian persecution.[92] Of course, this may well have been an exaggeration, but the persecution must have been sufficiently severe to have stayed in the collective memory of the Copts, who later called it 'the era of the martyrs'.[93]

In any case, it is highly improbable that our sources would list all the Christian martyrs in the Roman Empire. Many reports must have simply disappeared in the course of the ages, just as many classical writings have not survived the ravages of time. Moreover, during the Diocletian persecution the authorities not only looked for church treasures but also for Christian books, which they ritually burned on the spot or on the market.[94] Many documents of contemporary and previous martyrdoms,

---

[91] As shown by T. Barnes, *Constantine and Eusebius* (Cambridge MA and London, 1981) 154-55; note also Eusebius, *Hist. Eccl.* 8.7.1.

[92] Eusebius, *Hist. Eccl.* 8.8, 8.9.1.

[93] W. Clarysse, 'The Coptic Martyr Cult', in M. Lamberigts and P. van Deun (eds), *Martyrium in Multidisciplinary Perspective. Memorial Louis Reekmans* (Leuven, 1995) 377-95 at 381f.

[94] H. Gamble, *Books and Readers in the Early Church* (New Haven and London, 1995) 145-50; A. Luijendijk, *Greetings in the Lord. Early Christians and the Oxyrhynchus Papyri* (Cambridge MA, 2008) 207-10; M. Choat and R. Yuen-Collingridge, 'A Church with No Books and a Reader Who Cannot Write. The Strange Case of *P.Oxy*. 33.2673', *Bulletin American Society Papyrologists* 46 (2009) 109-38 at 130-35.

then, may well have perished in this manner. My observations do not imply a claim that there were many thousands of Christian martyrs: we simply do not have enough evidence to know the exact numbers. I only want to question the minimalism of Gibbon and his best known modern followers, Geoffrey de Ste. Croix and Robin Lane Fox,[95] as their computations are clearly more inspired by ideological convictions than by the available evidence.

It will be clear that in his famous two chapters Gibbon tried to understand the rise of Christianity, but in doing so also reacted to contemporary concerns and issues. In the latter respect, he was, in ways that are still being discussed,[96] an exponent of the Enlightenment. It will now also be clear that his enlightened views have influenced his analysis and not always for the better. Undoubtedly, his five causes are well worth considering and have led to a better understanding of Christianity's rise, but this is much less the case with Gibbon's discussion of the persecutions. It is not only that his main sources, in particular the French Jansenist Tillemont (1637-1698) and the German church historian Johann Lorenz Mosheim (1694-1755),[97] failed him in this respect;[98] it was also because he let his prejudices dominate the facts. This side of Gibbon did not es-

---

[95] De Ste. Croix, *Christian Persecution*, 68: 'The so-called Great persecution has been exaggerated in Christian tradition to an extent which even Gibbon did not fully appreciate', approvingly quoted by Lane Fox, *Pagans and Christians*, 596. For de Ste. Croix's Christian education and later anti-Christian convictions see the splendid portrait by R. Parker, 'Geoffrey Ernest Maurice de Ste. Croix 1910-2000', *Proceedings British Academy* 111 (2001) 447-78. For Lane Fox's views see his *The unauthorized version: truth and fiction in the Bible* (London, 1991).

[96] J. Pocock, 'The Enlightenment of Edward Gibbon', *Quaderni Storici* 94 (1997) 315-37 and 'The Re-description of Enlightenment', *Proceedings British Academy* 125 (2004) 101-17.

[97] Tillemont: D.P. Jordan, 'LeNain de Tillemont: Gibbon's "Sure-Footed Mule"', *Church History* 39 (1970) 483-502. Mosheim: I.483 note 105 (Chapter XV): 'In the history of the Christian hierarchy, I have, for the most part, followed the learned and candid Mosheim', cf. M. Mulsow *et al.* (eds), *Johann Lorenz Mosheim (1693-1755). Theologie im Spannungsfeld von Philosophie, Philologie und Geschichte* (Wiesbaden, 1997).

[98] See the fine study of O. Chadwick, 'Gibbon and the Church Historians', in Bowersock, *Edward Gibbon*, 219-31.

cape Theodor Mommsen, who was one of his great admirers.[99] Although being the superior ancient historian and a winner of the Noble Prize in Literature (1902), Mommsen recognised that he would be unable to surpass the *Decline and Fall* and therefore never published the final volume of his *Römische Geschichte* (1854-56). Fortunately, some decades ago, students' notebooks were discovered with Mommsen's lectures on the history of the Roman Empire. In it we read this judgment of the old grandmaster who, although not being a friend of Christianity in any way,[100] was not to be fooled: 'Gibbon ist noch das bedeutendste Werk, das je über die römische Geschichte geschrieben wurde ... In gelehrter Beziehung wird es überschätzt, auch ist es parteiisch, entgegengesetzt zu Tillemont, da Gibbon Atheist ist'.[101] This 'melancholy truth', to use one of his favourite expressions, means that Gibbon's impressive *Decline and Fall* always has to be used with care.

2 *Adolf von Harnack*

Although people doubting or denying the Christian truth are well attested from about 1500 onwards, they still lacked the conceptual tools to persuasively define their unbelief.[102] Yet irreligious speculation stead-

---

[99] B. Croke, 'Mommsen on Gibbon', *Quaderni di Storia* 32 (1990) 47-59; W. Nippel, 'Gibbon and German Historiography', in B. Stuchtey and P. Wende (eds), *British and German Historiography 1750-1950: traditions, perceptions, and transfers* (Oxford, 2000) 67-81 and 'Edward Gibbon und die Anfänge der modernen Althistorie'.

[100] S. Rebenich, *Theodor Mommsen und Adolf Harnack. Wissenschaft und Politik in Berlin des ausgehenden 19. Jahrhunderts* (Berlin and New York, 1997) 223-34.

[101] Th. Mommsen, *Römische Kaisergeschichte. Nach den Vorlesungs-Mitschriften von Sebastian und Paul Hensel*, ed. B. and A. Demandt (Munich, 1992) 430.

[102] The literature on the subject is large. See especially D. Wootton, 'Lucien Febvre and the Problem of Unbelief in the Early Modern Period', *J. Modern History* 60 (1988) 695-730 and 'New Histories of Atheism', in M. Hunter and D. Wootton (eds), *Atheism from the Reformation to the Enlightenment* (Oxford, 1992) 13-53; M. Gauna, *Upwellings. First expressions of unbelief in the printed literature of the French Renaissance* (Cranbury, 1992); G. Schwerhoff, 'Die alltägliche Auferstehung des Fleisches. Religiöser Spott und radikaler Unglaube um 1500', *Historische Anthropologie* 12 (2004) 309-37.

ily increased in subsequent times, and in the middle of the eighteenth century 'atheist' started to change from a term of abuse, as it had been since antiquity,[103] to a term of self-definition.[104] This development accelerated in the nineteenth century, when Christianity became ever more pluralistic,[105] and Berlin became one of the most secularized cities of Europe around 1900.[106] It is against this background that we have to look at Adolf von Harnack (1851-1930), our second scholar to be studied.

Harnack, who was ennobled in March 1914, was one of the most remarkable scholars of that brilliant period of German classical and patristic scholarship of the first decades of the twentieth century that was destroyed by the Nazis. He was born in Dorpat (Tartu) in Livonia (present-day Estonia and North Latvia), son of Theodosius Harnack (1817-1897), a staunch local Lutheran professor in theology who would always disapprove of his son's liberal Protestant views, and twin brother of Axel Harnack (1851-1888), a brilliant professor of mathematics in Dresden, whose name is still well known from the so-called 'Harnack inequality/ies'. His Baltic origin made Harnack a kind of outsider in Germany: he never joined a political party, and his liberal views kept him out of the Lutheran Church hierarchy. Yet, despite or perhaps because of this circumstance, he rose to become one of the most influential academics of Germany during the period 1890 to 1930.[107]

---

[103] Bremmer, 'Atheism in Antiquity', in M. Martin (ed.), *The Cambridge Companion to Atheism* (Cambridge, 2007) 11-26.

[104] K. Nowak, 'Logos atheos. Atheisten in der christlichen Gesellschaft des 18. Jahrhunderts zwischen Verfolgung und Duldung', in A. Dörfler-Dierken *et al.* (eds), *Christen und Nichtchristen in Spätantike, Neuzeit und Gegenwart* (Mandelbachtal and Cambridge, 2001) 151-79; G. Hyman, 'Atheism in Modern History', in Martin, *The Cambridge Companion to Atheism*, 27-46.

[105] For interesting points of view on this development see K. von Stuckrad, 'Die Esoterik in der gegenwärtigen Forschung: Überblick und Positionsbestimmung', *Zeitenblicke* 5 (2006) Nr. 1 = http://www. Zeitenblicke.de/ 2006/1/Stuckrad.

[106] H. McLeod, *Piety and Poverty: Working-class Religion in Berlin, London and New York, 1870-1914* (New York, 1996) 208.

[107] The biography by his gifted daughter remains indispensable: A. von Zahn-Harnack, *Adolf von Harnack* (Berlin, 1936), but the second edition of 1951 is to be read with B. Biester, 'Kritische Notizen zu Agnes von Zahn-Harnacks "Adolf von Harnack"', *Quaderni di storia* 27 (2001) 223-35. Helpful are also K. Nowak, 'Adolf

Harnack started his meteoric career in 1876 when he became *professor extraordinarius* in Leipzig. In 1888, after positions in Giessen and Marburg, he was already called to the Chair of Church History at the Friedrich-Wilhelms Universität in Berlin. His appointment was due to the influence on the young Wilhelm II by Friedrich Althoff (1839-1908),[108] the liberal Prussian civil servant who was mainly responsible for the glory of the German universities around 1900 and who often consulted Harnack for his appointments.[109] In 1890 Harnack was elected full member of the Prussian Academy of Sciences, and from 1903 to 1911 he was president of the Evangelisch-soziale Kongress, where he opposed *Gleichmacherei* but stressed the ethical and cultural aspects of working.[110] From 1905 to 1921 he was director of the Royal Library (nowadays Staatsbibliothek zu Berlin),[111] and from 1911 to 1930, at the explicit wish of Wilhelm II, he presided over the Kaiser-Wilhelm-Gesellschaft (renamed Max Planck Gesellschaft in 1946), then the leading institution in stimulating research in Germany.[112] In addition, he was

---

von Harnack. Wissenschaft und Weltgestaltung auf dem Boden des modernen Protestantismus', in idem (ed.), *Adolf von Harnack als Zeitgenosse*, 2 vols (Berlin and New York, 1996) 1.1-95 and C. Nottmeier, *Adolf von Harnack und die deutsche Politik* (Tübingen, 2004).

[108] Nottmeier, *Adolf von Harnack*, 104-16.

[109] B. vom Brocke (ed.), *Wissenschaftsgeschichte und Wissenschaftspolitik im Industriezeitalter. Das "System Althoff" in historischer Perspektive* (Hildesheim, 1991); F.W. Graf, 'Adolf Harnack zum "Fall Althoff". Zwei unbekannte Harnack-Briefe aus dem Dezember 1901', *Jahrbuch für Universitätsgeschichte* 1 (1998) 177-204; Rebenich, *Theodor Mommsen und Adolf Harnack*, 126-28; Nottmeier, *Adolf von Harnack, passim.*

[110] K. Nowak, 'Sozialpolitik als Kulturauftrag. Adolf von Harnack und der Evangelisch-soziale Kongress', in J.-C. Kaiser and W. Loth (eds), *Soziale Reform im Kaiserreich* (Stuttgart, 1997) 79-93; Nottmeier, *Adolf von Harnack*, 331-54.

[111] D. Fabian, 'Adolf von Harnack als Wissenschaftsorganisator und Bibliotheks-politiker', *Jahrbuch Preussischer Kulturbesitz* 37 (2000) 107-23; Nottmeier, *Adolf von Harnack*, 233-35, 262-67, 482-84; note also the reactions of Georg Wissowa (1859-1931) and Eduard Meyer (1855-1930) to Harnack's appointment: G. Audring (ed.), *Gelehrtenalltag. Der Briefwechsel zwischen Eduard Meyer und Georg Wissowa (1890—1927)* (Hildesheim, 2000) 184, 187, respectively.

[112] Nottmeier, *Adolf von Harnack*, 277-79.

active as *Wissenschaftsorganisator* in large research projects of the Berlin Academy, such as new editions of the Church Fathers,[113] and, last but not least, a prolific author with a bibliography of over 1500 items.[114]

Unique for a theologian, Harnack even had access to Emperor Wilhelm II.[115] Although he knew how to properly address him – *Allerdurchlauchtigster Grossmächtigster Kaiser und König! Allergnädigster Kaiser, König und Herr!* – Harnack was far from being the *Hoftheologe* his opponents made him out to be,[116] as he distanced himself from a theological letter by the emperor during the famous *Babel-Bibel Streit* ('Babel-Bible Controversy').[117] The result was that the two never again discussed theological or religious problems, but they stayed in touch, and when the British declared war to Germany on 4 August 1914, Harnack was asked for help in drafting the Emperor's *Call to the German People* of 6 August

---

[113] Von Zahn-Harnack, *Adolf von Harnack*, 254-64; Rebenich, *Theodor Mommsen und Adolf Harnack*, 55-94; S. Rebenich and C. Markschies, *Adolf von Harnack, Protokollbuch der Kirchenväter-Kommission der Preussischen Akademie der Wissenschaften 1897-1928* (Berlin and New York, 2000) and Rebenich, 'Der alte Meergreis, die Rose von Jericho und ein höchst vortrefflicher Schwiegersohn: Mommsen, Harnack und Wilamowitz', in K. Nowak and O.G. Oexle (eds), *Adolf von Harnack: Theologe, Historiker, Wissenschaftspolitiker* (Göttingen, 2001) 39-69 at 47-52.

[114] Cf. F. Smend, *Adolf von Harnack – Verzeichnis seiner Schriften bis 1930. Mit einem Geleitword und bibliographischen Nachträgen bis 1985 von J. Dummer* (Leipzig, 1990); for some additions see http://www.snts2005.uni-halle.de/ ST/ harnack/ biblio/ nachtraege. For literature see B. Biester, *Harnack-Bibliographie: Verzeichnis der Literatur über Adolf von Harnack: 1911 2002* (Erfurt and Munich, 2002), continued at http://anu.theologie.uni-halle.de/ST/ harnack/ biblio/ bibliographie?time_r=1.

[115] For Harnack and the imperial court see Von Zahn-Harnack, *Adolf von Harnack*, 339-52; R. vom Bruch, 'Adolf von Harnack und Wilhelm II.', in Nowak and Oexle, *Adolf von Harnack*, 23-37; Nottmeier, *Adolf von Harnack*, 233-62.

[116] J. Röhl, *Wilhelm II. Der Weg in den Abgrund, 1900-1941* (Munich, 2008) 562-66 at 565. Röhl's discussion suffers from an uncritical acceptance of Harnack's opponents' slandering.

[117] R.G. Lehmann, *Friedrich Delitzsch und der Babel-Bibel-Streit* (Freiburg and Göttingen, 1994), cf. Von Zahn-Harnack, *Adolf von Harnack*, 342-46; Nottmeier, *Adolf von Harnack*, 247-49.

1914. He was known for his superb formulations and could evidently not be missed at this special hour of need.[118]

Yet despite his many official functions, Harnack was above all both church historian and theologian or, perhaps better, a strongly historicizing theologian. In many ways he was a representative of the so-called *Kulturprotestantismus*, the movement that had accepted the modern world with its culture and politics, practised an active role within that world and stressed the autonomy of the individual,[119] even though Harnack always remained convinced of the 'Differenz zwischen Evangelium und Kultur'.[120] He set out his liberal theological views in the bestseller *Das Wesen des Christentums* (1900),[121] which was published at the same time as that other, even more successful bestseller, the Darwinistic *Die Welträtsel* of Ernst Haeckel. In their own distinctive ways, both these books touched a religious nerve in the Germany of the turn of the century.

Throughout his life Harnack opposed closed ideological and religious systems, and that explains why he was so interested in the study of the ancient Church, which he used as a benchmark to evaluate Protestantism, Roman-Catholicism and Judaism. His interest expressed itself in three magisterial books that still impress by their erudition: *Lehrbuch der Dogmengeschichte*, 3 vols (Tübingen, 1886-1890), *Geschichte der altchristlichen Literatur*, 2 vols (Leipzig, 1893-1904) and *Die Mission und Ausbreitung des Christentums* (Leipzig, 1902) – all within a 'Whig in-

[118] A(xel) von Harnack, 'Der Aufruf Kaiser Wilhelms II. beim Ausbruch des Ersten Weltkrieges', *Die neue Rundschau* 64 (1953) 613-14; J.C. O'Neill, 'Adolf von Harnack and the entry of the German state into war, July–August 1914', *Scottish Journal of Theology* 55 (2002) 1-18 (rather biased); Nottmeier, *Adolf von Harnack*, 378-84.

[119] F.W. Graf, 'Kulturprotestantismus. Zur Begriffsgeschichte einer theologiepolitischen Chiffre', in H.M. Müller (ed.), *Kulturprotestantismus* (Gütersloh, 1992) 21-77 and *Der Protestantismus* (Munich, 2006) 61-117.

[120] K. Nowak, 'Theologie, Philologie und Geschichte. Adolf von Harnack als Kirchenhistoriker', in Nowak and Oexle, *Adolf von Harnack*, 189-237 at 237.

[121] The book has often been reprinted, but the best edition is now A. von Harnack, *Das Wesen des Christentums*, ed. C.-D. Osthövener (Tübingen, 2005); see also W. Kinzig, 'Harnack heute. Neuere Forschungen zu seiner Biographie und dem "Wesen des Christentums"', *Theologische Literaturzeitung* 126 (2001) 473-500.

terpretation of German Protestantism'.[122] It is the last book to which we now will turn.

Die *Mission und Ausbreitung* is a relative small book – at least for Harnack. Its first edition counted 561 pages, but the fourth and standard edition of 1924 was already 1000 pages. This was the result of both reprinting earlier studies and the continuing collection of more primary evidence – additions that did not enhance the readability of the book. It does not help either that Harnack distrusted 'grand narratives' and did not have Gibbon's eye for lively details and the individuality of his protagonists, as his friend Mommsen had to point out to him.[123] But Harnack tried to be as clear as possible in the *Mission und Ausbreitung* and refrained from using specialized terminology and cross-sections of his material;[124] instead he opted for thematic *Längsschnitte* which made his argument more accessible and readable.[125]

Harnack was stupendously learned, and his book contains much more material than most modern scholars of early Christianity seem to realize, as he had literally read all available texts in all possible languages. As he proudly stated in the preface to the fourth edition: 'nachrühmen darf ich dem Werk, dass es so gut wie keine Hypothesen enthält, sondern Tatsachen zusammenstellt'. Although this statement betrays a certain methodological *naïveté*, the *Mission und Ausbreitung* is one more illustration of Harnack's remarkable powers of memory, concentration and organisation. These are even the more impressive as his family life does

---

[122] For a brief introduction to each of these three books see Nowak, 'Theologie, Philologie und Geschichte', 192-207.

[123] Mommsen had read the first edition of the *Mission und Ausbreitung* and made many oral and written comments (954 n. 1), cf. von Zahn-Harnack, *Adolf von Harnack*, 277-78; Nowak, 'Theologie, Philologie und Geschichte', 204. For Mommsen's friendship with Harnack see Harnack's funeral oration for Mommsen in Nowak, *Adolf von Harnack als Zeitgenosse*, 2.1530-39 (1903[1]); Von Zahn-Harnack, *Adolf von Harnack*, 264-71; W.M. Calder III and R. Kirstein, 'Agnes Von Zahn-Harnack's Forgotten Essay on Mommsen', *Classical World* 94 (2000) 39-46; Rebenich, 'Der alte Meergreis', 53-64; W.M. Calder III and R. Kirstein (eds), *«Aus dem Freund ein Sohn». Theodor Mommsen und Ulrich von Wilamowitz-Moellendorff, Briefwechsel 1872-1903*, 2 vols (Hildesheim, 2003) 2.488.

[124] Von Zahn-Harnack, *Adolf von Harnack*, 358f.

[125] Nowak, 'Theologie, Philologie und Geschichte', 204f.

not seem to have suffered that much from all his activities. Harnack did not mind his children using his study as a playground or even playing the piano in an adjacent room, and always dedicated the evenings to his family and social obligations in accordance with his rule: 'in meinem Hause wird nach 8 Uhr nicht mehr gearbeitet'.[126] Which modern scholar could say the same!

It is obvious that we cannot discuss 1000 pages in one lecture, and we will therefore concentrate on the main lines of Harnack's argument regarding the rise of Christianity. Admittedly, he uses many theological arguments in his book, but I shall try to avoid these, as they will not be acceptable to most modern readers. I will also not enter into a discussion of Harnack's analysis of the Gospels and *Acts*, as it is rather speculative and does not contribute much towards our main theme. Finally, although the *Mission und Ausbreitung* has often been reprinted, there hardly is any secondary literature that discusses it in some detail, and in many ways we are moving into unknown territory.[127]

Like Gibbon with his Chapter XV, Harnack (1-2) began his book by rejecting a theological explanation for Christianity's success ('not all have faith')[128] and by summarizing four causes that are clearly less secu-

---

[126] See the charming sketch of his family life in Von Zahn-Harnack, *Adolf von Harnack*, 280-93.

[127] In addition to Harnack's presentation of his own book in *Theologische Literaturzeitung* 27 (1902) 640-43, see L.M. White, 'Adolf Harnack and the "Expansion" of Early Christianity: A Reappraisal of Social History', *Second Century* 5 (1985-86) 97-127; S.J.D. Cohen, 'Adolph [sic] Harnack's "The Mission and Expansion of Judaism": Christianity Succeeds Where Judaism Fails', in B.A. Pearson (ed.), *The Future of Early Christianity* (Minneapolis, 1991) 163-69; C. Markschies, *Warum hat das Christentum in der Antike überlebt?* (Leipzig, 2004) 36-41; Nowak, 'Theologie, Philologie und Geschichte', 203-07; the preface and postface by M. Tardieu and P. Maraval to A. von Harnack, *Mission et expansion du christianisme aux trois premiers siècles*, tr. J. Hoffmann (Paris, 2004) i-xxvi, 761-66, respectively; I. Henderson, 'Mission and Ritual: Revisiting Harnack's "Mission and Expansion of Christianity"', in Henderson and G. Oegema (eds), *The Changing Face of Judaism, Christianity, and Other Greco-Roman Religions in Antiquity* (Gütersloh, 2006) 34-56.

[128] These words of (Deutero-)Paul (2 *Thessalonians* 3.2) are also quoted in *Das Wesen des Christentums*, 88.

lar than Harnack seems to have thought: 1) the Christian religion with its Church is the 'unbounded and therefore perfected Jewish religion' but also its *scharfe Antithese*; 2) the Christian religion with its Church is not only the perfection and dissolution (*Aufhebung* in the Hegelian sense) of Oriental-Greek syncretism and polytheism with its sacrificial practices, but also of pagan philosophy of religion, with which it successfully competed, unlike other religions; 3) the Christian religion with its Church is the great moral movement that concludes, democratizes and popularizes the ethical work (*die ethische Arbeit*) of paganism and Judaism. Although it recognized the state, it placed itself above it both ethically and as an episcopal theocracy, and 4) the Christian religion with its Church is the historical realisation of God's revelation. The Christians constituted a fraternal community above all peoples and the state; as such, this community could also oppose the state. The rest of the book elaborates these four theses.

Harnack divided the *Mission und Ausbreitung* into four books, the *first* of which deals with the problem of the external and internal conditions for the expansion of Christianity (5-110). Having noted the importance of the Roman Empire with its well organised infrastructure, he focused on the Jews and argued that they constituted a considerable part of the population of the Empire, which thus created favourable conditions for the Christian mission (5-13). The missionary impulse of the Jews should not be underestimated and was an important source of inspiration for the Christian mission (14-23). Although Jesus still concentrated on the Jews alone, he had already distanced himself from the nationalistic Pharisees by preaching that everybody, not just the Jews, were to be the adherents of his message. However, his was not yet a programme for a mission to the whole world (39-40). Recently, these ideas have become increasingly contested,[129] and not without reason. We have no idea how many Jews there were in the Roman Empire. Earlier calculations were totally built on sand, and contemporary scholars are agnostic about the number.[130] In addition to 'normal' converts, there were

[129] For a more detailed summary of Harnack's argument see W. Kinzig, *Harnack, Marcion und das Judentum* (Leipzig, 2004) 98-102.

[130] A. Wasserstein, 'The number and provenance of Jews in Graeco-Roman antiquity: A note on population statistics', in R. Katzoff (ed.), *Classical Studies in Honor of David Sohlberg* (Ramat Gan, 1996) 307-17; W. Ameling, 'Die jüdischen Ge-

different types of sympathizers with the Jews, such as God-fearers and proselytes,[131] but the meagre evidence available hardly supports the idea of Jewish missionary activity among the Gentiles,[132] the nature of which is not well elucidated by Harnack. Yet the Jews had clearly become receptive to Gentile sympathizers, and Paul, although not being the first 'Christian missionary' (53), may well have been inspired by that development; we simply do not know.

Harnack also discussed the hostility of the Jews towards the Christian mission. Admittedly, it is extremely difficult to separate fact from fiction in the polemics between Jews and Christians, but he surely exaggerated greatly by writing that the Jews sought to annihilate (*auszurotten*) the Palestinian congregations and to silence the Christian missionaries, by ascribing with near certainty the Neronian persecution to the Jews, and by seeing the Jews in the back- or foreground of nearly every other persecution (64-67). Although he opposed the rejection of the Old Testament and noted that the rejection of their Jewish roots by non-Jewish Christians was an injustice almost unprecedented (76),[133] Harnack argued that 'viewed from a higher standpoint' the Jews had dealt the death-blow to their own existence by their rejection of Jesus, whereas in their place the

---

meinden im antiken Kleinasien', in R. Jütte and A.P. Kustermann (eds), *Jüdische Gemeinden und Organisationsformen von der Antike bis zur Gegenwart* (Vienna, 1996) 29-55 at 30 on Asia Minor: 'es ist nur mein Eindruck nach inschriftlichen und archäologischen Quellen, dass ihr Bevölkerungsanteil unter 5% lag'; W. Scheidel, *Debating Roman Demography* (Leiden, 2001) 1-81 at 62.

[131] B. Wander, *Gottesfürchtige und Sympathisanten* (Tübingen, 1998); S.J.D. Cohen, *The Beginnings of Jewishness* (Berkeley, Los Angeles, London, 1999) 140-74; M. Görg, 'Woher kommt der "Proselyt"?', *Biblische Notizen* 103 (2000) 9-10 (Egyptian background of the term); W. Ameling, *Inscriptiones Judaicae Orientis* II (Tübingen, 2004) 16-20 (complicated meaning of the term 'God-fearer'); D.-A. Koch, 'The God-fearers between facts and fiction', *Studia theologica* 60 (2006) 62-90.

[132] M. Goodman, *Mission and Conversion: Proselytizing in the Religious History of the Roman Empire* (Oxford, 1994); R. Riesner, 'A Pre-Christian Jewish Mission?', in J. Ådna and H. Kvalbein (eds), *The Mission of the Early Church to Jews and Gentiles* (Tübingen, 2000) 211-50 (with an excellent *Forschungsgeschichte*).

[133] For Harnack's increasing reservations regarding the normativity of the Old Testament see Kinzig, *Harnack*, 98-102; Nottmeier, *Adolf von Harnack*, 485f.

Christians had appropriated the whole tradition of Judaism. Thus, in the end, non-Jewish Christianity completed a long-standing process within Judaism – its transformation into a proper world religion (76-77).[134]

Harnack's relationship to contemporary Judaism is not easy to evaluate, as we cannot escape looking at his writings with our knowledge of the terrible Nazi years that followed. Although he opposed racism and anti-Semitism,[135] he clearly had only a limited interest in contemporary Judaism and took little notice of the works of Jewish scholars.[136] For his knowledge of Jews and Palestine at the time of Jesus, Harnack mainly relied on the non-Jewish scholars Julius Wellhausen (1844-1918) and Emil Schürer (1844-1910), neither of whom was an anti-Semite, but both of whom took a dim view of Judaism at the time of Jesus.[137] On the other hand, we should not forget that although Harnack's judgments on, for example, the Pharisees strike us as extremely prejudiced, they were also shared by some contemporary liberal Jews.[138] Was Harnack anti-Jewish? Even that would go too far, but he did keep very friendly contacts with notorious anti-Semites, such as Houston Stewart Chamberlain (1855-1927).[139] In the end, his (lack of a) relationship to Judaism and the Jews remains problematic, and this shadow side of Harnack cannot be overlooked.[140]

---

[134] The notion of 'world religion' was relatively new at the time: it was invented by C.P. Tiele (1830-1902) in, probably, 1864, cf. Bremmer, 'Methodologische en terminologische notities bij de opkomst van de godsdienstgeschiedenis in de achttiende en negentiende eeuw', *Nederlands Theologisch Tijdschrift* 57 (2003) 308-20 at 317-18; C. Auffarth, '"Weltreligion" als ein Leitbegriff der Religionswissenschaft im Imperialismus', in U. van der Heyden and H. Stoecker (eds), *Mission und Macht im Wandel politischer Orientierungen* (Stuttgart, 2005) 17-36.

[135] Von Zahn-Harnack, *Adolf von Harnack*, 221; Kinzig, *Harnack*, 98-102; Nottmeier, *Adolf von Harnack*, 240-1, 256-8 (racism).

[136] C. Wiese, *Wissenschaft des Judentums und protestantische Theologie im wilhelminischen Deutschland* (Tübingen, 1999) 131-39.

[137] Wellhausen and Schürer: Kinzig, *Harnack*, 172-3 (with bibliography).

[138] Nottmeier, *Adolf von Harnack*, 486.

[139] Kinzig, *Harnack*, 207-97; Nottmeier, *Adolf von Harnack*, 254-59.

[140] For an excellent discussion of Harnack's views see Kinzig, *Harnack*, 155-205, 299-302, who is considerably more subtle than Cohen, 'Adolph Harnack's "The Mission and Expansion of Judaism"'.

Having analysed the origins and first stages of the Christian mission, Harnack then turned to the contents and attractions of the missionary preaching of this 'simple religion' (113), the *second* book of his *Mission und Ausbreitung* (111-331). Originally, as he suggested, the preaching consisted of a brief eschatological statement: 'The kingdom of God is at hand, repent, as the judgement comes with and before the kingdom' (115). The very fact that in earlier editions the second part of the statement is missing shows how fragile the evidence is for such early Christian statements. Yet, as recent history has taught us, simple slogans such as 'New Deal', 'Jesus loves you' or 'Power to the people' do mobilize people. Comparable early Christian statements were portable, easy to communicate and helped to constitute a kind of unity across all kinds of borders: social, religious and political.[141]

Subsequently, Harnack (inspired by Gibbon?) argued that the new preaching could be reduced to five points: 1) The one living God, the creator of heaven and earth; 2) Jesus the Saviour; 3) the forgiving of sins through baptism; 4) the resurrection and 5) ascetic self-control (119-20). From these points the preaching of the resurrection (120-21) really drew pagan attention, as we have already seen (§ 1). Yet the main proof for most of these statements are some passages from the *Acts of Paul and Thecla* (120 n. 1), which dates from the later second century at the earliest.[142] The fact that somewhat later Harnack connected these five points with the ideas of retribution and the saving cross (124) as well as a strict ethical life (124-28) shows how difficult he found it to reduce the early preaching to a specific core. The theologian in him needed such a systematisation, but the sources hardly support him.

Other aspects are less debatable and are often mentioned by modern historians of early Christianity. The healing of body and soul by Christ, which gave him the epithet *Medicus*, 'Physician' (129-50),[143] as well as

[141] Hopkins, *World full of Gods*, 98; W. Keane, *Christian Moderns. Freedom and Fetish in the Missionary Encounter* (Berkeley, Los Angeles, London, 2007) 69.

[142] Bremmer, 'The Apocryphal Acts: Authors, Place, Time and Readership', in J.N. Bremmer (ed.), *The Apocryphal Acts of Thomas* (Leuven, 2001) 149-70 at 153f.

[143] D. Knipp, *'Christus Medicus' in der frühchristlichen Sarkophagskulptur. Ikonographische Studien zur Sepulkralkunst des späten vierten Jahrhunderts* (Leiden, 1998); R. von Bendemann, 'Christus der Arzt', *Biblische Zeitschrift* 54 (2010) 36-53.

the exorcising of demons (151-70) undoubtedly did produce converts,[144] but we have no idea to what extent they were the main aspects that impressed them. Exorcism was one of the legacies of Second Temple Judaism to Christianity,[145] and the Christians successfully exported faith in the efficacy of the practice – called the 'awful ceremony' by Gibbon (I.472) – to the rest of the Roman Empire: the exorcist even became a minor member of the Christian clergy already relatively early on. Unlike the Jews, though, the Christians often dramatized exorcism as a battle against pagan gods or heretics like Simon Magus, as in the apocryphal *Acts of Peter*. The ritual not only healed patients but also demonstrated the superiority of the Christian God.[146]

Charity (170-220) and the belief in miracles (220-39) had already been noted by Gibbon (§ 1), although Harnack (946) mentions his name only once. However, he collected much more material than Gibbon and stressed the Christian claim that miracles were not performed just for impressing people but precisely for moral regeneration and ethical improvement.[147] That is why Christian authors often observed that, unlike pagan wonderworkers, the Christians performed their miracles without hocus pocus and never accepted money for their miracles.[148] It was the

---

[144] MacMullen, *Christianizing the Roman Empire*, 28-29 with n. 9.

[145] G. Bohak, *Ancient Jewish Magic* (Cambridge, 2008) 88-114; add K. Berthelot, 'Guérison et exorcisme dans les textes de Qumrân et les évangiles', in P. Boulhol *et al.* (eds), *Guérisons du corps et de l'âme* (Aix-en-Provence, 2006) 135-48; E. Eshel, 'Jesus the Exorcist in Light of Epigraphic Sources', in J.H. Charlesworth (ed.), *Jesus and Archaeology* (Grand Rapids, 2006) 178-85; R. Leicht, 'Mashbia' Ani 'Alekha: Types and Patterns of Ancient Jewish and Christian Exorcism Formulae', *Jewish Studies Quarterly* 13 (2006) 319-43.

[146] K. Thraede, 'Exorzismus', in *RAC* 7 (Stuttgart, 1969) 44-117; Brown, *Society and the Holy*, 123-6; Lane Fox, *Pagans and Christians*, 327-30; Z. Ritoók, 'Horkos und exorkismos', in U. Luft (ed.), *The Intellectual Heritage of Egypt* (Budapest, 1992) 503-08; R. Kotansky, 'Exorcistic Amulets', in M. Meyer and P. Mirecki (eds), *Ancient Magic and Ritual Power* (Leiden, 1995) 243-77.

[147] For Harnack's own (sceptical) views regarding miracles see *Das Wesen des Christentums*, 23-26.

[148] Bremmer, 'Magic in the *Apocryphal Acts of the Apostles*,' in J.N. Bremmer and J.R. Veenstra (eds), *The Metamorphosis of Magic from Late Antiquity to the Early Modern Period* (Leuven, 2002) 51-70 at 70.

Christian life style and care for others that indeed is regularly attested as influencing conversion (231-34).

Moreover, Christianity was unique in that it displayed reverence for sorrow and suffering. This reverence was nourished by the ideals of gentleness and humbleness, as stressed in Jesus' words 'Take my yoke upon you and learn from me; for I am gentle and humble in heart' (*Matthew* 11.29). Yet these lofty ideals did not last. Harnack concluded his chapter on 'the religion of spirit and of power' with the observation that routine and convention gradually stripped these ideals from their inner spirit and made them positively repulsive (237-38). It is interesting to note that this sociological insight, which does not yet occur in the first edition, is rather unique in Harnack's work but would return in a different form in Max Weber's ideas about the *Veralltäglichung*, 'routinization', of charisma. Weber knew Harnack personally, and the latter had given him the second edition of his *Mission und Ausbreitung* in return for Weber's study of *Die protestantische Ethik und der 'Geist' des Kapitalismus* (1905); moreover, both had been together at the 1904 *Congress of Arts and Science* in St Louis.[149] Yet there cannot be a connection, as the term *Veralltäglichung* does not occur in Weber's work before about 1913 and can hardly have been invented by him,[150] although in German publications of the first decades of the twentieth century it occurs only in a Weberian context.[151] It is more likely that Harnack somehow was inspired by the discussion about charisma with the legal historian Rudolf Sohm

[149] See Weber's letter of thanks (5 February 1906) in M. Weber, *Briefe 1906-1908 = Max Weber Gesamtausgabe II/5*, ed. M.R. Lepsius and W.J. Mommsen (Tübingen, 1990) 32-3; J. Radkau, *Max Weber* (Munich, 2005) 368-73 (St Louis), 495-6 (letter); H. Lehmann, *Die Entzauberung der Welt* (Göttingen, 2009) 86-7. For Weber's letter of thanks for the third edition (4 December 1915) see M. Weber, *Briefe 1915-1917 = Max Weber Gesamtausgabe II/9*, ed. G. Krumeich and M.R. Lepsius (Tübingen, 2000) 200f.

[150] It was already used by B. Christiansen, *Philosophie der Kunst* (Berlin, 1912) 128. For Weber see M. Weber, *Wirtschaft und Gesellschaft = Max Weber Gesamtausgabe I/22.2*, ed. H. Kippenberg (Tübingen, 2001) 214, 228, 250, 307 and *I/22.4*, ed. E. Hahnke (Tübingen, 2005) 625.

[151] The term remained so rare that it is still lacking in J. and W. Grimm, *Deutsches Wörterbuch 25: V-Verzwunsen* (Leipzig, 1956).

(1841-1917), who had been the first to put 'charisma' on the scholarly agenda.[152]

Why did the Christians believe what they did? On the basis of which authority did they believe? This clearly is a problem that had not occurred to Gibbon, but which Harnack tried to elaborate in some detail (239-58). He noticed that the philosopher Celsus reproached the early Christians of being rather simple people, who accepted the Christian teaching in blind faith and without any proof. However, this pagan criticism should be recognized for the rhetorical ploy it was, as it was expressed precisely at the moment that Christian intellectuals became visible in the wider Roman society.[153] Yet the Christian faith was not wholly blind; it appealed to certain authorities such as, first, the apostle Paul and, later, the Church and the episcopate. Harnack clearly disapproved of this development as it went against his own view that historically developed Church teaching should always be open to criticism. He had more sympathy for the early Christian apologists, whom he calls the 'rationalists of the supernatural' (246). The term is not unsuitable, as these intellectuals criticized the mythological traditions of the Greek gods,[154] which could no longer stand up to rigorous rationalist investigations, just as Christian mythological traditions, like the story of the creation or of Jesus' birth, no longer persuade many people in the West.

---

[152] R. Sohm, *Kirchenrecht I* (Munich, 1892), cf. P. Haley, 'Rudolph Sohm on Charisma', *Journal of Religion* 60 (1980) 185-97, overlooked by Radkau, *Max Weber*, 601-02; E. Hahnke, in *Max Weber Gesamtausgabe I/22.4*, 38-41.

[153] G. Schöllgen, 'De ultima plebe. Die soziale Niedrigkeit der Christen als Vorwurf ihrer Gegner', in Hutter, *Hairesis*, 159-71; H.R. Seeliger, 'Litteratulus christianus: Beobachtungen und Bemerkungen zum Bildungsgrad der antiken Christen', *Theologische Quartalschrift* 183 (2003) 297-312; A. Fürst, *Christentum als Intellektuellen-Religion* (Stuttgart, 2007).

[154] M.J. Edwards *et al.* (eds), *Apologetics in the Roman Empire: Pagans, Jews, and Christians* (Oxford, 1999); A. Wlosok *et al.*, *L'apologétique chrétienne gréco-latine à l'époque prénicénienne* (Vandoeuvres-Geneva, 2004); M. Friedowicz, *Apologie im frühen Christentum* (Paderborn, 2006³); A. Klostergaard Petersen, 'The Diversity of Apologetics: From Genre to a Mode of Thinking', in A.-C. Jacobsen *et al.* (eds), *Critique and Apologetics* (Frankfurt, 2009) 15-41; L. Roig Lanzillotta, 'Christian Apologists and Greek Gods', in J.N. Bremmer and A. Erskine (eds), *The Gods of Ancient Greece* (Edinburgh, 2010) 442-64.

From a ritual point of view, Harnack interestingly saw the two sacraments of baptism and eucharist as important means of supporting the preaching (248-58). He even considered them substitutes for animal sacrifice. Undoubtedly, the latter ritual was on the way out in Late Antiquity, and the spirit of the times was thus favourable to Christianity in this respect. Yet the Christians not only used sacrificial terminology when speaking about Christ's crucifixion in the eucharist,[155] but they also kept or adapted ancient sacrificial rites at the margins of Christendom.[156] Apparently, the break with their environment and their Jewish past was not always as sharp as one might have thought.[157]

The origins of the two sacraments have often been debated,[158] but it is more important to observe that they helped to create solidarity in the community and unity in Christianity as a whole. Especially the eucharist must have impressed some non-Christians, as both Justin and Tertullian noted the presence of eucharist-like bread in Mithraic rites, and bread and grapes are sometimes significantly displayed in the Mithraic

---

[155] E. Thomassen, 'The Reception of Greco-Roman Religious and Cultic Terminology in Judaism and Christianity, with Special Reference to Sacrificial Terminology', in D. Brakke *et al.* (eds), *Beyond Reception. Mutual Influences between Antique Religion, Judaism, and Early Christianity* (Frankurt, 2006) 137-53 at 143-53.

[156] E. Kovaltchuk, 'The Encaenia of St Sophia: Animal Sacrifice in a Christian Context', in V. Baranov and B. Lourié (eds), *Scrinium IV: Patrologia Pacifica* (St Petersburg, 2008) 161-203 (with thanks to Guy Stroumsa); note also F. Oinas, *Studies in Finnic-Slavic Folklore Relations* (Helsinki, 1969) 193-201.

[157] S. Bradbury, 'Julian's pagan revival and the decline of blood sacrifice', *Phoenix* 49 (1995) 331-56; M.-Z. Petropoulou, *Animal Sacrifice in Ancient Greek Religion, Judaism, and Christianity, 100 BC to AD 200* (Oxford, 2008); G. Stroumsa, *The End of Sacrifice* (Chicago and London, 2009) 56-83.

[158] Kinzig and Wallraff, 'Das Christentum des 3. Jahrhunderts', 332-56 (baptism); W.M. Gessel, 'Organisation, Formen des Gemeindelebens', in Zeller, *Christentum I*, 301-30 at 326-30 (eucharist); M.E. Johnson, 'Christian Initiation', in Harvey and Hunter, *Oxford Handbook of Early Christian Studies*, 693-710; D. Sheerin, 'Eucharistic Liturgy', *ibidem*, 711-43; N. Bériou *et al.* (eds), *Pratiques de l'eucharistie dans les Églises d'Orient et d'Occident (Antiquité et Moyen Age)*, 2 vols (Paris, 2009).

holy meal or banquet scene, the event following the tauroctony.[159] Harnack did not note these parallels but would have welcomed them, as he thought that Christianity had profited from the *alten Mysterienweisheit* (256, 272). Yet the connections between Christianity and the mysteries are mainly terminological and have often been overestimated;[160] in fact, some mystery cults clearly derived ideas from Christianity itself in the course of time.[161] Students of Late Antiquity should always keep in mind that pagans and Christians lived side by side and borrowed from one another when that seemed to be advantageous.

Another source of authority was the book (289-99), although, according to Harnack, Christianity never became a 'religion of the Book' like Islam. The expression shows that he knew its coinage by Max Müller in 1873,[162] but it also shows Harnack's interest in Islam. In fact, as a student he had already boldly argued that the Islam was 'a transformation of Jewish religion, which itself had already been transformed by Gnostic Jewish Christianity, on the ground of the Arabs, through a great prophet'.[163] The book Harnack mentioned was the Old Testament, and Egyptian pa-

---

[159] Justin, *I Apol.* 66.4, *Dialog.* 70.1, 78.6; Tertullian, *De praescriptione haereticorum* 40, cf. P. Beskow, 'Tertullian on Mithras', in J. Hinnells (ed), *Studies in Mithraism* (Rome, 1994) 51-60; E. Sauer, *Classical Review* 57 (2007) 497.

[160] C. Riedweg, *Mysterienterminologie bei Platon, Philon und Klemens von Alexandrien* (Berlin and New York, 1987); D. Zeller, 'Mysterien/Mysterienreligionen', in *Theologische Realenzyklopädie* 23 (1994) 503-26; C. Auffarth, '"Licht vom Osten": Die antiken Mysterienkulte als Vorläufer, Gegenmodell oder katholisches Gift zum Christentum', *Arch. f. Religionsgesch.* 8 (2006) 206-26; Thomassen, 'The Reception of Greco-Roman Religious and Cultic Terminology', 140-43.

[161] Harnack, *Mission und Ausbreitung*, 940 n. 1, overlooked by Bremmer, *Rise and Fall of the Afterlife*, 52-55, who is quoted by J. Alvar, *Romanising Oriental Gods: Myth, Salvation and Ethics in the Cults of Cybele, Isis and Mithras Religions in the Graeco-Roman World*, tr. and ed. R. Gordon (Leiden, 2008) at 292 n. 338, but neglected at 383-421.

[162] F.M. Müller, *Introduction to the Science of Religion* (London, 1873) 102-22.

[163] During his *Lizentiaten-Promotion* in 1874 he had defended the thesis: *Muhamedanismum rectius quam Manichaeismum sectam Christianam esse dixeris*: A. Harnack, *Lehrbuch der Dogmengeschichte*, 4 vols (Tübingen, 1909^4) 2.529-38 at 529 and 537, cf. A. von Scheliha, *Der Islam im Kontext der christlichen Religion* (Münster, 2004) 74-84.

pyri have since confirmed his opinion. They show that *Psalms* was by far the most popular part of the Old Testament among the early Christians, followed at some distance by *Genesis* and *Exodus*, whereas from the New Testament *Matthew* and *John* were wider read than the other gospels or Paul. With the exception of the *Shepherd* of Hermas (§ 1), these books were also much more popular among early Christians than the so-called apocryphal writings, which should give food for thought to those who stress the great importance of those writings for early Christianity.[164]

Books did become more important in religions in Late Antiquity, but Judaism tenaciously stuck to its scrolls whereas, regarding its Scriptures, Christianity moved with the times and changed to the codex, the forerunner of our modern book, in the earlier second century.[165] This technological advantage must have made carrying round the Word much easier and was adopted by the Manichaeans, a really missionary religion that originated in Mesopotamia in the third century AD and faded away in southern China in the fifteenth and sixteenth centuries. The relatively small size of the codex made early Christianity and Manichaeism true 'religions of the paperback'![166]

But could the early Christians read these books? Keith Hopkins (1934-2004) has argued that by 100 AD most Christian communities did not have 'among them a single sophisticated reader or writer'.[167] Yet such an assumption does not explain the many letters written and preserved in the period of early Christianity (379-89). Although only a small mi-

---

[164] L. Hurtado, *The Earliest Christian Artifacts: Manuscripts and Christian Origins* (Grand Rapids and Cambridge, 2006) 15-41; Martinez, 'Papyri and Early Christianity', 593-99.

[165] E.A. Meyer, 'Roman *Tabulae*, Egyptian Christians, and the Adoption of the Codex', *Chiron* 37 (2007) 295-347; Bagnall, *Early Christian Books*, 70-90; Bremmer, 'From Holy Books to Holy Bible: an Itinerary from Ancient Greece to Modern Islam via Second Temple Judaism and Early Christianity', in M. Popović (ed.), *Authoritative Scriptures in Ancient Judaism* (Leiden, 2010) 327-60.

[166] S.N.C. Lieu, *Manichaeism in Central Asia and China* (Leiden, 1998); Stroumsa, *End of Sacrifice*, 28-55 (growing importance of books for late antique religion) at 43 (who uses the expression for Christianity).

[167] K. Hopkins, 'Christian Number and Its Implications', *J. Early Christian Studies* 6 (1998) 185-226 at 213.

nority could read and own books,[168] people like Paul, the pseudo-Pauls, Clement and Ignatius surely expected their letters to be studied and circulated, and everything we know seems to point to Christianity being a movement connected and maintained by the written word, in other words, being a textual community.[169] This was an important difference from Graeco-Roman religion and cults like those of Isis, Mithras or Cybele. Nowhere do we see that their followers felt connected with 'fellow believers' in other places in the Roman Empire. Even though we can look at early Christianity as a collection of local communities, one of its strengths must have been the feeling of an empire-wide community sustained by epistolary and other contacts.

Harnack concluded his *second* book with a brief epilogue on Christianity as a syncretistic religion (324-31). In his opinion, it had taken over too many elements from Judaism, the mysteries and pagan philosophy of religion.[170] Yet, unlike some of his contemporaries, Harnack was quite careful in not claiming a pagan origin for specific elements of early Christianity, such as Sunday, the eucharist or the Virgin birth. In Harnack's time, syncretism carried a pejorative meaning and suggested a mixing of 'pure' Christianity with Greek or Oriental religious elements. However, nowadays many scholars are rather reticent in using the term, as it has become increasingly realized that all religions constantly borrow elements from other religions

---

[168] For our scarce information regarding the costs of copying books see E. Dekkers, 'Des prix et du commerce des livres à l'époque patristique', in M. Geerard *et al.* (eds), *Opes Atticae: Miscellanea philologica et historica = Sacris Erudiri* 13 (Steenbrugge, 1990) 99-115; S. Mratschek, '*Codices vestri nos sumus*. Bücherkult und Bücherpreise in der christlichen Spätantike', in A. Haltenhoff and F.-H. Mutschler (eds), *Hortus Litterarum Antiquarum: Festschrift fur Hans Armin Gärtner zum 70. Geburtstag* (Heidelberg, 2000), 369-80; Bagnall, *Early Christian Books*, 50-69.

[169] Gamble, *Books and Readers in the Early Church*, 1-41.

[170] For ancient Christianity's self-definition as a philosophy see most recently G.H. van Kooten, 'Is Early Christianity a Religion or a Philosophy? Reflections on the Importance of 'Knowledge' and 'Truth' in the Letters of Paul and Peter', in Dijkstra, *Myths, Martyrs, and Modernity*, 393-408; W. Löhr, 'Christianity as Philosophy: Problems and Perspectives of an Ancient Intellectual Project', *Vigiliae Christianae* 64 (2010) 160-88.

or ideologies; there are no 'pure' religions.[171] Harnack used this syncretistic Christianity as a foil for his own plea for a simple Christianity that concentrated on the living God as our Father and on the representation of Jesus in the Gospels. We no longer need such a foil, and it surely is unthinkable that Christianity became triumphant without any accommodation to its pagan environment. Yet each case of possible pagan influence has to be looked at individually, and earlier scholars, such as the great Hermann Usener (1834-1905),[172] were regularly too hasty in discovering polytheistic elements, driven as they were by ideological motives.

In his *third* book Harnack looked at the missionaries, their methods and the counter-movements (332-528). His exposition of terms such as 'apostle', 'prophet' and 'teacher' is learned (332-77),[173] but it does obscure the fact that we can hardly mention any active missionaries in the second and third centuries.[174] Harnack had realized this too, but thought that the martyrs made many converts (377-78, 397, 505), which is unlikely, as we will see shortly (§ 3). Thus, somewhat in passing, he concluded that it was the moral life of many Christians and the influence of women (§ 3) that were the main reasons for the expansion of Christianity (378). Yet Harnack may have underrated the influence of teaching to the newly converted. Early Christianity obliged those who wanted to join and be baptized to follow religious instruction, the so-called catechumenate

---

[171] R. Gordon, 'Synkretismus I', in *Der Neue Pauly* 11 (2001) 1151-55; C. Markschies, 'Synkretismus. V. Kirchengeschichtlich', in *Theologische Realenzyklopädie* 32 (2001) 538-52; C. Auffarth, 'Synkretismus. IV. Antike', in *Religion in Geschichte und Gegenwart*⁴, vol. 7 (Tübingen, 2004) 1962-64; M. Tardieu, 'Les facettes du syncrétisme: méthodologie de la recherche et histoire des concepts', in G. Veinstein (ed.), *Syncrétismes et hérésies dans l'Orient seldjoukide et ottoman (XIVe-XVIIe s.)* (Paris, 2005) 3-16; P. Xella, '"Syncrétisme" comme catégorie conceptuelle', in C. Bonnet *et al.* (eds), *Les religions orientales dans le monde grec et romain: cent ans après Cumont (1906-2006)* (Brussels and Rome, 2009) 134-50 (with detailed bibliography).

[172] Bremmer, 'Hermann Usener', in W.W. Briggs and W.M. Calder III (eds), *Classical Scholarship: A Biographical Encyclopedia* (New York, 1990) 462-78.

[173] For the teachers see now R. Kany, 'Lehrer', in *RAC* 22 (2008) 1091-1131.

[174] As is well observed by Lane Fox, *Pagans and Christians*, 282 and R. Hvalvik, 'In Word and Deed: The Expansion of the Church in the pre-Constantinian Era', in Ådna and Kvalbein, *Mission of the Early Church*, 265-87.

(390-405).[175] Whereas Greek and Roman religion had no organised religious education,[176] the instruction of the early Christians must have been a clear advantage in discussions with those interested in the new faith and an important element of their religious capital.

Equally unsatisfactory is Harnack's discussion of the importance of the local congregations (445-59). He rightly noticed that such congregations were unique and new in the ancient world. Yet it does not really become clear from his discussion why they would attract outsiders. The reason must have been one of the most important aspects of Christian social capital: the processes of bridging and bonding.[177] The early Christians met in private houses, as is well illustrated by the so-called Apocryphal Acts of the Apostles. In the *Apocryphal Acts of John* (46) of about 150 AD, the apostle John preached in the house of a prominent citizen on Sunday, and in the only slightly later *Acts of Paul and Thecla*, Paul preached in Iconium in the house of Onesiphorus (5-7) and in Ephesus in the house of Aquila and Priscilla.[178] Such meetings in small groups must have promoted the bridging of social distances, as it enabled the poor to mix with the rich and the slaves with the free, which will have contributed to their self-esteem and well-being.[179]

---

[175] Kinzig and Wallraff, 'Das Christentum des 3. Jahrhunderts', 339-48; M. Metzger and H. Brakmann, '*Katechumenat*', in *RAC* 20 (2003) 497-574; Luijendijk, *Greetings in the Lord*, 115-18 (papyrological evidence); P. Gavrilyuk, *Histoire du catéchuménat dans l'église ancienne* (Paris, 2008).

[176] Bremmer, 'The Family and Other Centres of Religious Learning in Antiquity', in J.W. Drijvers and A.A. MacDonald (eds.), *Centres of Learning* (Leiden, 1994) 29-38; A. Mehl, 'Religiöse Erziehung und Unterweisung in der griechischen Antike', in M. Liedtke (ed.), *Religiöse Erziehung und Religionsunterricht* (Bad Heilbrunn, 1994) 67-86.

[177] For this terminology see R. Wuthnow, 'Religious Involvement and Status-Bridging Social Capital', *J. Scientific Study Religion* 41 (2002) 669-84. Here and elsewhere I make freely use of Bremmer, 'Social and Religious Capital of the Early Christians'.

[178] R. Kasser and P. Luisier, 'Le papyrus Bodmer XLI en édition princeps. L'épisode d'Éphèse des *Acta Pauli* en copte et en traduction', *Muséon* 117 (2004) 281-384.

[179] H.-J. Klauck, *Hausgemeinde und Hauskirche im frühen Christentum* (Stuttgart, 1981); C. Markschies, *Zwischen den Welten wandern: Strukturen des antiken Christentums* (Frankfurt, 1997) 187-92; P. Lampe, *From Paul to Valentinus* (Min-

Another kind of bridging must have been that of the gender gap. There is plenty of evidence that early Christian women could move much more freely among men than their pagan counterparts. We already find 'women of high standing' among Paul's followers in *Acts* (13.50, 17.12) and well-to-do businesswomen in the *Shepherd* of Hermas (*Mand.* 5.2.2) and, as time went on, there must have also been a steadily growing number of poor women. One of the attractions of Christianity, both 'orthodox' and 'heretical', clearly was the opportunity for better educated and intellectually curious women to mix with intellectual men.[180] The *Passion of Perpetua* gives a moving account of such a close tie between the spiritual leader Saturus and the young woman Perpetua, both of whom were executed on 7 May 203.[181] In other words, even if we have little concrete information, everything we know about early Christianity indicates that the early congregations were relatively egalitarian and supplied important bridging and bonding opportunities.

Harnack also concluded his *third* book with a brief epilogue (526-28). He noted how the Christian mission started with Paul and some nameless apostles, who preached the one God, the coming judgement and Jesus Christ. This mission already had virtually ended at the time of Origen. But instead there now existed a powerful Church with priests, sacraments, doctrines and a philosophy of religion, which exerted a missionary influence by its simple existence. This Church represented the consummation of all previous religions, and this Church inevitably had to become the world religion that would eventually end all other religions and draw people to it as to a magnet. Its universal spirit that encompassed the entire life of people guaranteed its victory. It had

---

neapolis, 2003) 359-65. For possible Jewish roots (house synagogues) see C. Claussen, *Versammlung, Gemeinde, Synagoge* (Göttingen, 2002) 37-9.

[180] Harnack, *Mission und Ausbreitung*, 601-02; Bremmer, 'Why Did Early Christianity Attract Upper-class Women?', in A.A.R. Bastiaensen *et al.* (eds), *Fructus centesimus, Mélanges G.J.M. Bartelink* (Steenbrugge and Dordrecht, 1989) 37-47; Stark, *Rise of Christianity*, 95-128. Unfortunately, E.A. Clark, 'Thinking with Women: the Uses of the Appeal to "Woman" in Pre-Nicene Christian Propaganda', in Harris, *Spread of Christianity*, 43-51 limits herself to an analysis of discourse.

[181] See now J.N. Bremmer and M. Formisano (eds), *Perpetua's Passions* (Oxford, 2011).

to prevail, as in its core it was something simple (Harnack's favourite theme!): 'God as the Father, the Judge and the Redeemer, made known in and through Jesus Christ' (528). These apologetic and theological words speak for themselves. They show us Harnack the theologian, not the church historian, and they will not persuade those who do not share his convictions.

Having dedicated the first three books to the Christian *Mission*, in the *fourth* and final book Harnack described the *Ausbreitung* by presenting an astonishingly learned survey of all the passages that mention the numerousness of the early Christians (529-52), the main dates of the missionary history (552-58) and Christianity's spread among the upper classes (559-68), the court (568-77), the military (577-88) and women (589-611) as well as some pages on the actual church buildings. This survey is still valid in most cases, except regarding the aristocracy and the church buildings. Prosopography has shown that the male aristocracy became converted only gradually to Christianity,[182] and archaeology has unearthed many more examples of early Christian church architecture.[183] Even though Harnack himself realised that he could not keep up with all the specialists of local and regional archaeological discoveries (620 note 1), he still added an amazingly detailed survey of all places in the Roman Empire where Christians are attested until 325 AD (618-927), 'heretical' Churches, such as the Marcionites and Novatianists, included (928-32), and illustrated by maps that he himself had designed.[184] It is

---

[182] W. Eck, 'Christen im höheren Reichsdienst im 2. und 3. Jahrhundert? Zu zwei Thesen Th. Klausers', *Chiron* 9 (1979) 449-64 and 'Religion und Religiosität in der soziopolitischen Führungsschicht der Hohen Kaiserzeit', in W. Eck (ed.), *Religion und Gesellschaft in der römischen Kaiserzeit. Kolloquium zu Ehren von Friedrich Vittinghoff* (Cologne, 1989) 15-51; T.D. Barnes, 'Statistics and the Conversion of the Roman Aristocracy', *J. Roman Studies* 85 (1995) 135-47; M. Salzman, *The Making of a Christian Aristocracy: Social and Religious Change in the Western Roman Empire* (Cambridge MA and London, 2002).

[183] S. de Blaauw, 'Kultgebäude C', in *RAC* 22 (2008) 227-393; K. Bowes, *Private Worship, Public Values, and Religious Change in Late Antiquity* (Cambridge, 2008) *passim*; R. MacMullen, *The Second Church: Popular Christianity, A.D. 200-400* (Atlanta, 2009) 117-41.

[184] Von Zahn-Harnack, *Adolf von Harnack*, 358.

hard to conceive of anybody today who would even make an attempt at starting such a survey.[185]

Harnack concluded his magisterial book with some interesting observations on the differing numbers of Christians in the Empire; there were many more in the East than the West. He also stressed that Christianity grew with an amazing speed (956-7), even though he remained careful regarding the actual numbers and suggested 3-5% in the cities by the middle of the third century (946-956). In the end, for Harnack, we cannot specify which element of early Christianity, be it Christ, monotheism or its strict morals – to name a few of the many possible factors – was decisive, but the main causes were its preaching of the living God, and its adaptation to, but also its struggle against, contemporary pagan religion and Greek philosophy. Those who were simple found something simple; those who were sublime something sublime. As a world religion, Christianity offered what was necessary but also what everybody wanted (957-8).

Although deeply impressed by his erudition, most modern readers will lay down Harnack's book with ambivalent feelings. There are several good reasons for that reaction. First, most modern scholars do not share his theological convictions and teleological views of Christian history. Second, Harnack's picture is largely sketched out without much reference to the pagan *Umwelt*. It is not only that Harnack had a limited interest in Judaism, but he also does not seem to have been all that curious about the pagan world in which Christianity originated.[186] Third,

---

[185] Harnack has not been replaced by Lane Fox, *Pagans and Christians*, 265-93; G. Clark, 'Third-century Christianity', in A.K. Bowman *et al.* (eds), *The Cambridge Ancient History XII* (Cambridge, 2005²) 589-671 at 589-616 or by the surveys in Harvey and Hunter, *Oxford Handbook of Early Christian Studies*, 283-386 (several authors).

[186] MacMullen, *Paganism in the Roman Empire*, 206 n. 16 even states: 'Among its thousands of references to sources ... I can find not one to a pagan source and hardly a line indicating the least attempt to find out what non-Christians thought and believed'. Although MacMullen is quoted with approval by Stark, *Rise of Christianity*, 193, this is a completely misguided remark, as Harnack studied the pagan qualification of Christianity as a *genus tertium* (281-89), analysed the arguments of Celsus and Porphyry (513-25) and referred to the collection of material in his *Geschichte der altchristlichen Literatur bis Eusebius I* (Leipzig, 1893)

the more facts Harnack collected, the less readable the book became. Yet, more importantly, all these facts impede a better understanding of the connection between them and their religious, social and political background as well as the structures and dynamics of early Christianity itself. In the very last words of his book (958 n. 1), Harnack praised Max Weber's famous study on the already mentioned *Protestantische Ethik*, and in the introduction he praised Ernst Troeltsch (2-3 note 1); both were the star sociologists of religion of his time. Yet there is virtually no trace of influence of their work in his *Mission und Ausbreitung*,[187] and this makes Harnack's presentation intellectually rather unsatisfactory. In that respect, his book was already out of date in 1924. Fourth and finally, the attentive reader cannot fail to note that Harnack hardly ever manages to come up with specific Christian missionaries despite all his erudition, which probably did not overlook a single early Christian text.[188] Now the nineteenth century was *the* age of the Christian mission; by 1900, there were more than 2000 missionaries in China and more than 100,000 in Africa alone.[189] Can it be that Harnack was looking in the wrong direction and had been misled by the nature of the Christian mission of his own time? In order to answer that question we shall now turn to our last work.

3 *Rodney Stark*

A century after the first publication of Harnack's work, the Western world looks very different in religious respects. Growing consumerism and individualisation have caused a strong decline of the Christian Churches in most of Europe and, if to a much lesser degree, in the United States. Even if the precise reasons for this secularisation still have to be properly

---

865-76 (513 note 1). For the pagan objections to Christianity see now Levieils, *Contra Christianos* and J. Engberg, *Impulsore Chresto. Opposition to Christianity in the Roman Empire c. 50-250 AD* (Frankfurt, 2007).

[187] Nowak, 'Theologie, Philologie und Geschichte', 206.

[188] The few examples left are disposed of by Reinbold, *Propaganda und Mission*, 286-96.

[189] C.A. Bayly, *The Birth of the Modern World, 1780-1914* (Oxford, 2004) 343-51; J. Osterhammel, *Die Verwandlung der Welt. Eine Geschichte des 19. Jahrhunderts* (Munich, 2009) 1261-68.

analysed for many countries,[190] it seems clear that the 1960s were a religious watershed in several ways.[191] Increasingly, personal empowerment has become more important than the salvation of the soul, especially in America but more and more also in Europe.[192] An epiphenomenon of this development has been the rise of a number of so-called New Religious Movements, a collective term for all kinds of new cults and religions since, especially, the 1960s.[193] One of the best known students of these Movements is the American sociologist of religion Rodney Stark (1934-), who was born in Jamestown, North Dakota, where he was baptised and confirmed as a Lutheran. He started his academic career at the University of California, Berkeley,[194] and having been Professor of Sociology and of Comparative Religion at the University of Washington for more than thirty years, Stark became Distinguished Professor of the Social Sciences at Baylor University (Texas) in 2004. He is a highly productive scholar with a sharp mind, an easy pen, which is undoubtedly due to his early work as a journalist, and a willingness to tackle larger issues. Whereas in the earlier part of his career he often published together with other scholars, in the last decade Stark has been singlehandedly flooding the market with about a book a year on subjects ranging from Mormons, the crusades and monotheism to the origins of religion.[195] Yet his best

[190] For a recent survey see D. Pollack, 'Säkularisierung – Konzept und empirische Befunde', in H. Kippenberg *et al.* (eds), *Europäische Religionsgeschichte*, 2 vols (Göttingen, 2009) 1.61-86. For the rise of the term 'secularisation' see Bremmer, 'Secularization: Notes Toward a Genealogy', in H. de Vries (ed.), *Religion: Beyond a Concept* (New York, 2008) 432-37, 900-03.

[191] Two important studies: H. Mcleod, *The Religious Crisis of the 1960s* (Oxford, 2007); C. Brown, *The Death of Christian Britain* (London, 2009²).

[192] Bremmer, 'From Salvation to Empowerment. European Notes on Contemporary American Religion', *First Draft: The Newsletter of the Getty Research Institute* 6 (2007) 10-15.

[193] See, for example, J.R. Lewis (ed.), *The Oxford Handbook of New Religious Movements* (Oxford, 2004); P.B. Clarke (ed.), *Encyclopedia of New Religious Movements* (London and New York, 2006).

[194] A.L. Mauss, 'Rodney Stark: The Berkeley Years', *J. Scientific Study Religion* 29 (1990) 362-66.

[195] For a list consult: http://en.wikipedia.org/wiki/Rodney_stark#Books.

known book among the wider public is most likely *The Rise of Christianity* of 1996.

With this work we enter a world totally different from our previous scholars. Both Gibbon and Harnack were experts on the ancient world, if each in their own way. Our last iconic figure has no credentials in this respect. Yet the choice of subject is typical of Stark's scholarly daring or, as some would prefer, recklessness. By his own confession he is not a New Testament scholar or a historian. His aim is to contribute 'better social science – better theories and more formal methods of analysis, including quantification wherever possible and appropriate' (xii). Stark, then, is the complete opposite of Harnack, who was proud of having offered virtually no hypotheses in his work. Moreover, whereas the latter read all Christian texts in the original, Stark has to depend on translations. Whereas Harnack was mostly facts, Stark is mostly theory. Whereas Harnack was rather cautious, Stark is nothing but adventurous. Finally, with its stress on agency and rationality, Stark's favourite theoretical perspective, Rational Choice Theory,[196] is a typically modern approach, with nomothetic ambitions that override all the complicating specificities of context, culture and history.[197] Despite these objections we prefer Stark and his approach above the only other candidate as a contemporary iconic figure, Robin Lane Fox, whose 1986 *Pagans and Christians* is rather mainstream in its argument, however well written and well informed.

Unfortunately, there are very few studies dealing with Stark's analysis of the rise of Christianity. Although the book was widely and favourably reviewed in social science journals, the classical and patristic world has been rather shy in confronting his arguments, with the honourable exception of special issues of the *Journal of Early Christian Studies* (1998) and the *Religious Studies Review* (1999).[198] So let us see to what extent the book is really innovative and holds up to historical scrutiny.

---

[196] See, for example, R. Stark and R. Finke, *Acts of Faith* (Berkeley, Los Angeles, London, 2000).

[197] Thus, rightly, J.M. Bryant, *Sociology of Religion* 58 (1997) 191-95 at 192.

[198] But see B. Pearson, 'On Rodney Stark's Foray into Early Christian History', *Religion* 29 (1999) 171-6; S. Spence, *The Parting of the Ways: the Roman Church as a Case Study* (Leuven, 2004) 209-44; G. Lundskow, 'The Concept of Choice in the Rise of Christianity: A Critique of Rational Choice Theory', in W.S. Goldstein (ed.), *Marx, Critical Theory, and Religion* (Leiden, 2006) 223-48 (amateurish).

Stark starts with the arithmetic of Christian growth, a problem that immediately catches attention (4-13). Following a suggestion of E.R. Goodenough (1893-1965)[199] that 10 percent of the Empire was Christian at the time of Constantine and accepting the conventional number of 60,000,000 inhabitants at that time, he assumes that there were 1,000 Christians by 40 AD and about 6,300,000 by 300 AD, as 'Christians were so numerous that Constantine found it expedient to embrace the church (5)'.[200] This would give an average rate of growth of about 40 percent per decade, which comes close to the 43 percent per decade of the Mormons.[201] Unfortunately, the argument is highly contentious. Unlike the Christians, the Mormons could operate in a world with much better transport and more advanced media to popularise their message. Moreover, as a highly insightful review of Stark's book notes: 'it strains all credulity that this or any other religious movement experiences a constant and linear rate of conversion over long periods of social-historical change'.[202] As regards the actual numbers, it seems unlikely that there were already 1,000 followers of Christ in such a short time after his execution. On the other hand, the fact that Tacitus (*Ann.* 15.44) mentions a *multitudo ingens* of martyrs in Rome during the Neronian persecution surely suggests a sizeable number of Christians by 65 AD, an impression confirmed by the late first-century *1 Clement* (6). And indeed, if there had not been quite a few Christians in such a big city as Rome, how could they have been recognised, arrested and executed?

It is not so different with the adduced number of Christians by 300 AD, which is equally arbitrary and not based on any certain ancient evidence. The fact that the most recent authoritative discussion wavers between 60 and 100 million inhabitants for the Roman Empire as a whole shows that all computations are based on quicksand.[203] As MacMul-

[199] E.R. Goodenough, *The Church in the Roman Empire* (New York, 1931) 39, 41.

[200] Even Gibbon (I.725-27, 738-44) had already been considerably more sophisticated in his discussion of Constantine, cf. J. Straub, 'Gibbons Konstantin-Bild', in P. Ducrey (ed.), *Gibbon et Rome à la lumière de l'historiographie moderne* (Geneva, 1977) 159-85, reprinted in his *Regeneratio imperii* II (Darmstadt, 1986) 252-82.

[201] Stark is an acknowledged expert on the Mormons, cf. his *The Rise of Mormonism* (New York, 2005).

[202] Bryant (n. 197), 192.

[203] Scheidel, *Debating Roman Demography*, 63-4.

len observes, the number of 8 to 12 percent is indeed quite normally found but justified by nobody.[204] Stark also overlooks the problem that the Roman Empire was unevenly Christianised, as the Latin West, but also parts of Greece and the Balkan, had few Christian congregations,[205] which means that the percentage growth elsewhere must have been even much higher than the postulated 40 percent.

Stark is more convincing when he discusses conversion (13-21). As a young scholar in the early 1960s, he became involved in research on conversion in connection with the Unification Church, the 'Moonies'. Its main findings were that people become involved in New Religious Movements through their social networks and get seriously attached to the doctrines of their new faith only after their conversion, whereas people who are deeply committed to one faith do not join another. Although subsequent research among Dutch adolescents has argued that the new group also offers them a new perspective on life and so liberates them from entrapment in their own problems, the resulting article has held up very well and is something of a classic in Conversion Studies.[206] Strangely enough, Stark only briefly discusses the application of his findings to early Christianity, as if the matter speaks for itself. But in the first decades of the Christian movement, there cannot have been that many networks available to the travelling missionaries. That is undoubtedly why in *Acts* Luke shows us Paul visiting synagogues to preach the new faith.[207] Networking presupposes existing circles of friends and acquaintances, and these would have been much more available in the

---

[204] MacMullen, *Second Church*, 102 note 18 with the evidence.

[205] Harnack, *Mission und Ausbreitung*, 946-55; Lane Fox, *Pagans and Christians*, 311; MacMullen, *Second Church*, 112.

[206] J. Lofland and R. Stark, 'Becoming a World-saver: a Theory of Conversion to a Deviant Perspective', *American Sociological Review* 30 (1965) 862-74; W. Kox *et al.*, 'Religious Conversion of Adolescents: Testing the Lofland and Stark Model of Religious Conversion', *Sociological Analysis* 52 (1991) 227-40. For recent evaluations of the various conversion models see the contributions by S. Bruce, D. Hak, H. Gooren and H. Zock in J.N. Bremmer *et al.* (eds), *Paradigms, Poetics and Politics of Conversion* (Leuven, 2006) 1-58.

[207] For observations on the linguistic situation Paul encountered among the Jews see the stimulating essay by D. Mendels and A. Edrei, *Zweierlei Diaspora. Zur Spaltung der antiken jüdischen Welt* (Göttingen, 2010) 78-82.

second and third centuries. Yet the insight is valuable, and we will have to come back to it in our final conclusion.

Having thus briefly looked at the conversion process, Stark briskly moves on to the social basis of the early Christians (29-47). Here he advances the thesis that if the early Church was like other cult movements, it must have been based on the more privileged classes (33). Gibbon still came close to modern Marxist explanations by stating that 'minds afflicted by calamity and the contempt of mankind, cheerfully listen to the divine promise of future happiness' (I.510), but Harnack (559-68) already knew better. However, Stark's confidence should not mislead us into thinking that we know much about the young Christian congregations. A major hindrance for a more precise idea of the early Christian social composition is the fact that Paul avoids situating people within the Roman ranking system. That is why we can say only a few words about first-century Corinth and Rome, whereas we have no idea whatsoever about the social composition of all other congregations. It is only by 200 AD that we are able to gather a bit more information about the largest cities of the Roman Empire, such as Rome, Carthage and Alexandria, but otherwise we have no idea.[208] Yet Stark's view might well be right. Given the taxes they had to pay and the instruction they received in the synagogues, it probably was not the poorest of the poorest Jews who were meeting in the synagogues where the first Christian missionaries preached.[209] Moreover, the overrepresentation of Roman names in Paul's

---

[208] Schöllgen, *Ecclesia sordida?*, to be read with the critical observations by H.R. Seeliger, 'Überlegungen zur Soziologie des frühen Christentums', in M.-B. von Stritzky and C. Uhrig (eds), *Garten des Lebens. Festschrift W. Cramer* (Altenberge, 1999) 261-74 and 'Das Netzwerk der *communio*. Überlegungen zur historischen Soziologie des antiken Christentums und ihrer Bedeutung für die Ekklesiologie', in B.J. Hilberath (ed.), *Communio – Ideal oder Zerrbild von Kommunikation?* (Freiburg, 1999) 19-38; Schöllgen, 'De ultima plebe'; Judge, *First Christians*, 501-12.

[209] The subject is underresearched, but see *Acts* 6.9 (Synagogue of the Freedmen); J.M.G. Barclay, *Jews in the Mediterranean Diaspora* (Edinburgh, 1996) 414-18 (taxes and instruction); Ph. Harland, *Associations, Synagogues, and Congregations* (Minneapolis, 2003) 200-10. For the early synagogues see also A. Runesson *et al.*, *The Ancient Synagogue from its Origins to 200 C.E.: A Source Book* (Leiden, 2008).

letters suggests a number of Roman citizens who would not be members of the lowest strata either.[210] That is all there is to say in this respect.

But where did the main converts come from? Stark advances the audacious thesis that Jews not only provided the initial basis for Church growth and continued to do so as late as the fifth century, but also that Jewish Christianity was still significant in the fifth century (49-71). In support of his case, Stark offers not a single piece of evidence from antiquity that Jews saw Christianity as their pathway to assimilation in the Empire, but he reasons from similarities with nineteenth-century Reform Judaism (53-54, 69), which tried to assimilate to Gentile society but also to keep some ties with its old faith. However, it is hard to believe that Jews would have opted to become Christians in a time of persecutions, as this would have defeated the purpose of their conversion. The evidence we have also speaks against such conversions. Even in the first century, Jews comprised hardly more than 25 to 30 per cent of the believers connected with the Pauline mission and churches,[211] and we hear virtually no more about Jewish converts in the next two centuries when 'original Jewish tradition took on its own life within circles of Gentile Christians'.[212] Consequently, we cannot, as Skarsaune does, extrapolate from the Roman data to a general 10 to 20 per cent of Jewish Christians from the total of Christians in the Empire by 250 AD. There simply is no evidence or likelihood for such a high number.[213] In addition, although

---

[210] See the interesting onomastic investigations of Judge, *First Christians*, 553-67 ('The Roman Base of Paul's Mission', 2005[1]).

[211] All recent studies agree that Jews were very quickly a minority: Lampe, *From Paul to Valentinus*, 69-79; D.C. Sim, 'How many Jews became Christians in the first century?: the failure of the Christian mission to the Jews', *Hervormde Teologiese Studies* 61 (2005) 417-40; for the percentage, R. Hvalvik, 'Named Jewish Believers Connected with the Pauline Mission', in O. Skarsaune and R. Hvalvik (eds), *Jewish Believers in Jesus: The Early Centuries* (Peabody, 2007) 154-78 at 178 and 'Jewish Believers and Jewish Influence in the Roman Church until the Early Second Century', *ibidem*, 179-216 at 215.

[212] Lampe, *From Paul to Valentinus*, 79 (quote and 2 Jewish converts at the end of the second century).

[213] *Contra* O. Skarsaune, 'The History of Jewish Believers in the Early Centuries – Perspectives and Framework', in Skarsaune and Hvalvik, *Jewish Believers in Jesus*, 745-81 at 770. Note Skarsaune's personal investment in the subject as mentioned

the belief in the existence of so-called (groups of) Jewish Christians has long been popular in scholarly circles, the outcome of the most recent investigation in all the available evidence is rather sobering. When we look critically at Christian heresiologists, we are left with hardly any well defined groups of Jewish Christians at all.[214]

On the other hand, it is clear that Judaism was still alive and well in Late Antiquity,[215] as synagogues now began to dot the landscape, especially in the eastern half of the Roman Empire. Here many monumental buildings could be found, and dedicatory inscriptions, specific iconographic programs and apses for the instalment of Torah shrines would leave no visitor in any doubt that he had entered a typically Jewish building. This surprising rise of the Late Antique synagogue cannot be separated from the accelerating Christianisation of the Empire under its Christian emperors. It is as if the Jews wanted to affirm their own identity when faced with the increasing pressure of the Christian majority.[216] Moreover, in a few places Judaism still proved to be attractive to Christians. Antioch is a well known case through the sermons of John Chrysostom,[217] and a more recently published, late fourth- or early fifth-

---

on 780-1.

[214] See the studies by Skarsaune on the Ebionites, Kinzig on the Nazoreans and Af Hällström/Skarsaune on Cerinthus and other Jewish Christian groups in Skarsaune and Hvalvik, *Jewish Believers in Jesus*, 419-502; Boyarin, 'Rethinking Jewish Christianity'.

[215] For Judaism in the Eastern half of the Roman Empire see most recently the survey by F. Millar, 'Christian Emperors, Christian Church and the Jews of the Diaspora in the Greek East, CE 379-450', *Journal of Jewish Studies* 55 (2004) 1-24, which updates G. Stemberger, 'Juden', in *RAC* 19 (1998) 160-228 at 185-91.

[216] Ameling, 'Die jüdischen Gemeinden', 53-54 and 'Die jüdische Diaspora Kleinasiens und der "Epigraphic Habit"', in J. Frey *et al.* (eds), *Jewish identity in the Greco-Roman World* (Leiden, 2007) 253-82 at 279-81; G. Stemberger, *Juden und Christen im spätantiken Palästina* (Berlin and New York, 2007), to be added to L.V. Rutgers, *Making Myths. Jews in Early Christian Identity Formation* (Leuven, 2009) 79-115. For 'identity', a fairly slippery concept, see, to start with, P. Stachel, 'Identität: Genese, Inflation und Probleme eines für die zeitgenössischen Sozial- und Kulturwissenschaften zentralen Begriffs', *Arch. f. Kulturgesch.* 87 (2005) 395-425.

[217] H.I. Newman, 'Jerome's Judaizers', *J. Early Christian Studies* 9 (2001) 421-53;

century inscription from Aphrodisias shows that the local synagogue still attracted proselytes and God-fearers.[218] Although Jews occasionally converted in considerable numbers in Late Antiquity when forced by mob violence as, for example, on the island Minorca in 418 AD,[219] our limited evidence only points to Christian and pagan interest in Judaism, not to frequent conversions,[220] and certainly not to massive Jewish conversion to Christianity.

Stark is more persuasive in stressing the advantage of the Christians during epidemics, when they helped their fellow believers and thus survived to a larger degree than the pagan inhabitants of the Empire (73-94). As he rightly claims, non-Christians would not have been preached to regarding their duties of charity, and Christianity clearly had an advantage here, although it is unclear what this actually meant in practice. Numerical advantage is also part of Stark's discussion of the role of women in the rise of Christianity (95-128), as he argues that Christian opposition to abortion and infanticide, which was a Jewish legacy,[221] must have removed major causes of the gender imbalance among pa-

---

J. Hahn, *Gewalt und religiöser Konflikt* (Berlin, 2004) 139-89; R. Ziadé, *Les martyrs Maccabées: de l'histoire juive au culte chrétien. Les homélies de Grégoire de Nazianze et de Jean Chrysostome* (Leiden, 2007) 111-35; I. Sandwell, *Religious Identity in Late Antiquity. Greeks, Jews and Christians in Antioch* (Cambridge, 2007); Rutgers, *Making Myths*, 19-48, who all overlooked A. Hilhorst, 'Fourth Maccabees in Christian Martyrdom Texts', in C. Kroon and D. den Hengst (eds), *Ultima Aetas. Time, Tense and Transience in the Ancient World. Studies in Honour of Jan den Boeft* (Amsterdam, 2000) 107-21.

[218] Ameling, *Inscriptiones Judaicae Orientis II*, 71-112 (= no. 14); A. Chaniotis, 'The Conversion of the Temple of Aphrodite at Aphrodisias in Context', in J. Hahn *et al.* (eds), *From Temple to Church: Destruction and Renewal of Local Cultic Topography in Late Antiquity* (Leiden, 2008) 243-73 at 247-49.

[219] Severus of Minorca, *Letter on the Conversion of the Jews*, ed. S. Bradbury (Oxford, 1996); C. Ginzburg, *Il filo e le tracce* (Milan, 2006) 39-51 ('La conversione degli Ebrei di Minorca', 1996[1]).

[220] L.V. Rutgers, *The Hidden Heritage of Diaspora Judaism* (Leuven, 1998) 209-19.

[221] D. Schwartz, 'Did the Jews Practice Infant Exposure and Infanticide in Antiquity?', *Studia Philonica Annual* 16 (2004) 61-95; L.T. Stuckenbruck, *1 Enoch 91-108* (Berlin and New York, 2007) 390-1; D. Shanzer, 'Voices and Bodies: The Afterlife of the Unborn', *Numen* 56 (2009) 326-65.

gans (99). Yet how much impact this all had can only be anybody's guess. Moreover, Stark's claim that the sex ratio in Rome (130 males against 100 females) and elsewhere (140 against 100) was heavily male-biased, is wholly based on antiquated sources and methods. All we can say is that the sex-ratio in imperial Rome and elsewhere would have been more or less even.[222]

On the other hand, there is indeed general agreement among historians that women were overrepresented in early Christianity.[223] How can we explain this? There must have been several causes depending on which category of women one belonged to: Stark mentions wives, widows and brides. For wives, one reason would have been the relative safety provided by the Christian ideal of monogamy. We are perhaps so used to the contemporary nuclear families that we do not realise that, from a global anthropological perspective, strict social monogamy has always been fairly rare. Christian attitude in this respect, which drew upon its Jewish roots, was a real exception in its surrounding world.[224] Undoubtedly, some women had married pagan men. Stark (114) concedes that 'there is no abundance of direct evidence' (an understatement!) that such marriages were widespread but, characteristically, still claims that they were an important factor in the conversions. Yet we have no idea if the women surplus was typical of the nubile ones or more widespread among the older ones. In fact, in several cases the conversion of the women led them to practise chastity, which may not always have helped the conversions of their husbands.[225]

The possibilities offered to women to realise their intellectual talents must have been another attraction to join Christianity, even if this

[222] W. Jongman, 'Slavery and the growth of Rome', in C. Edwards and G. Woolf (eds), *Rome the Cosmopolis* (Cambridge, 2003) 100-22; W. Scheidel, 'Human mobility in Roman Italy, II: The slave population', *J. Roman Studies* 95 (2005) 1-16. Hopkins, 'Christian Number', 206 notes that the larger the number of Christians, the more likely that their demographic composition will have reflected that of the larger population.

[223] Lane Fox, *Pagans and Christians*, 308-11.

[224] W. Scheidel, 'A Peculiar Institution? Greco-Roman Monogamy in Global Context', *History of the Family* 14 (2009) 280-91.

[225] Reinbold, *Propaganda und Mission*, 301-04.

sounds rather modern.[226] Moreover, in early Christian literature, starting with *Acts*, we regularly hear of rich widows who joined the Church and thus could act as patronesses of the small house-congregations. Their number must have been so important that the early Church created a special place for them in the ecclesiastical hierarchy, the so-called *ordo viduarum*, 'order of widows', just as other women could make an ecclesiastical career in the early Church, at least in the lower orders.[227] Even though the *ordo* gradually disappeared when more people joined the Church, it must have been important in the first two centuries. But the Church did not attract only rich widows. The care of poor widows and orphans was an important duty in ancient Israel, and the early Church preserved this part of its Jewish legacy. In a book which he wrote around 165 AD about the self-immolation of Peregrinus, the pagan satirist Lucian mentions that during his Christian period the philosopher was visited in prison by 'old crones, widows and orphans' (12), categories typical of the most vulnerable in the ancient world and not valued in pagan society.[228]

Stark also claims that Christian brides married much later than their pagan counterparts, but the most recent study of the age at marriage of women in the Roman Empire ruefully concludes that the demographic

---

[226] See above (§ 2) on intellectual Christian women.

[227] U. Eisen, *Women Officeholders in Early Christianity. Epigraphical and Literary Studies*, tr. L. Maloney (Collegeville, 2000); K. Madigan and C. Osiek, *Ordained Women in the Early Church. A Documentary History* (Baltimore and London, 2005) to be read with the review of I. Ramelli, *Orpheus* 28 (2007) 338-46; G. Macy, *The Hidden History of Women's Ordination. Female Clergy in the Medieval West* (Oxford, 2008), with the review by Ramelli, *Studi e Materiali di Storia delle Religioni* 74 (2008) 347-53.

[228] Widows: R. Bruno Siola, '*Viduae* e *coetus viduarum* nella Chiesa primitiva e nella normazione dei primi imperatori cristiani', in *Atti dell'Academia Romanistica Constantiniani: VIII convegno internazionale* (Naples, 1990) 367-426; Bremmer, 'Pauper or Patroness: The Widow in the Early Christian Church', in J.N. Bremmer and L.P. van den Bosch (eds), *Between Poverty and the Pyre. Moments in the History of Widowhood* (London, 1995) 31-57; G. Dunn, 'Widows and Other Women in the Pastoral Ministry of Cyprian of Carthage', *Augustinianum* 45 (2005) 295-307. Old women: Bremmer, 'The Old Women of Ancient Greece', in J. Blok and P. Mason (eds), *Sexual Asymmetry, Studies in Ancient Society* (Amsterdam, 1987) 191-215.

parameters of 'Roman marriage' remain exceedingly poorly known. There is something to say for girls marrying in their late teens, but even that suggestion is hard to substantiate.[229] There simply is not enough evidence about pagan women, let alone early Christian ones. Here as elsewhere, Stark's statistics, however impressive to the uninitiated, are once again totally built on quicksand.[230]

Stark's most interesting chapter probably is his discussion of the martyrs (163-89). He rightly opposes previous answers to the question: What made them do it? Those answers usually departed from the premise that people opting for martyrdom were irrational. Stark, on the other hand, starts from the idea that individuals 'choose their actions rationally, including those actions which concern compensators' (= 'rewards that are otherwise not plausibly obtainable'). Rational choice, in his view, involves weighing the anticipated costs and benefits of actions (169). Although the suggestion that we should look at martyrs not as irrational beings but as people who may well have thought deeply about their choice is persuasive,[231] Christian martyrdom was not always a well-pondered, rational choice. Some people displayed their solidarity with the martyrs in an impulse and subsequently became martyred themselves.[232] Clearly, Stark's point of departure, Rational Choice Theory,

---

229 W. Scheidel, 'Roman funerary commemoration and the age at first marriage', *Classical Philology* 102 (2007) 389-402 at 402.

230 This is also true for his chapter on urbanization (129-45). As Karin Neutel points out to me, Stark's nonchalant treatment of the sources is well illustrated by a comparison of his population figures of major cities adduced in *The Rise of Christianity*, 131-32, and in *Cities of God* (San Francisco, 2006) 34-59. For example, without alerting the reader about the differences, Apamea counts 125,000 inhabitants in *Rise* but 37,000 in *Cities* (38), Antioch 150,000 in *Rise* but 100,000 in *Cities* (37), etc. The only valid point probably is the correlation between the existence of synagogues and Christianisation, but this is valid only for the first century.

231 That cannot be said about his notes on the number of martyrs (164, 179, 182): see the above discussion of Gibbon (§ 1).

232 See, for example, Justin, *II Apol.* 2.19-20; *Acts of Lyons and Vienne* 1.10, 49; *Acta Carpi* A, 42-44; *Passio Eupli* 1; Eusebius, *Hist. Eccl.* 8.9.5.

does not explain everything,[233] just as domestic violence or hate killings fall outside of that theoretical framework.[234]

But if Christian martyrdom was a rational choice, what benefits did the martyrs expect? Stark is not clear about these, but we can at least make three points. First, tracts advocating the value of martyrdom and testimonies about impressive martyrdoms were popular in the early Church, and martyrs were officially remembered from an early stage onwards,[235] as, for example, Augustine did in his sermons about Perpetua and Felicitas.[236] Such treatises and commemorations must have helped to sustain the faith of the believers under attack. Similarly, contemporary suicide bombers are honoured on posters, murals, web sites and public exhibits, and imams dedicate sermons to commemorate their lives.[237] Second, those who had stayed steadfast during arrest or torture had gained a lasting reputation for the rest of their lives.[238] Third, Gibbon (I.545-46) had already noted that, unlike other Christians, martyrs

---

[233] For recent critiques see S. Bruce, *Choice and Religion: a critique of rational choice theory* (Oxford, 1999); Goldstein, *Marx, Critical Theory, and Religion*; J. de Jonge, *Rational and Moral Action. A Critical Survey of Rational Choice Theory* (Diss. Amsterdam, 2009).

[234] S. Atran, 'Genesis of Suicide Terrorism', *Science* 299 (2003) 1534-39 at 1536.

[235] H. Delehaye, *Les Passions des Martyrs et les genres littéraires* (Brussels, 1966^2) 11-59.

[236] D. Elm von der Osten, 'Perpetua Felicitas: Die Predigten des Augustinus zur Passio Perpetuae et Felicitatis', in Th. Fuhrer (ed.), *Die christlich-philosophischen Diskurse der Spätantike: Texte, Personen, Institutionen* (Stuttgart, 2008) 275-98; I. Schiller *et al.*, 'Sechs neue Augustinuspredigten. Teil 1 mit Edition dreier Sermones', *Wiener Studien* 121 (2008) 227-84 at 251-64 (Sermo 282 auct. edited by C. Weidmann).

[237] The importance of the community is emphasized in, among others, F. Khosrokhavar, *Les Nouveaux Martyrs d'Allah* (Paris, 2002); M. Sageman, *Understanding Terror Networks* (Philadelphia, 2004) and *Leaderless Jihad: Terror Networks in the Twenty-First Century* (Philadelphia, 2008); A. Moghadam, *The Globalization of Martyrdom: Al Qaeda, Salafi Jihad, and the Diffusion of Suicide Attacks* (Baltimore, 2008).

[238] B. Kötting, *Ecclesia peregrinans*, 2 vols (Münster, 1988) 1.122-44 (on the so-called *confessores*).

expected to go straight to heaven after their execution,[239] just as modern Islamic suicide bombers expect to go straight to Paradise and not to feel their wounds.[240]

Although a number of Christians chose to die for their faith, is it true that, as Gibbon (I.547) observed, 'on these melancholy occasions, there were many among the Gentiles who pitied, who admired, and who were converted'? Tertullian, who had dedicated a special treatise to martyrdom, certainly thought so and even famously stated: 'the blood of the Christians is the seed' (of the Church: *Apologeticum* 50); his opinion was shared by other early Christians.[241] Admittedly, the literature of the imperial era – Roman, Greek and Jewish – was much interested in physical suffering and the power to endure it.[242] This ability to resist torture and suffering became an important feature in early Christian self-definition, as we can observe in Christian novels, such as the *Acts of Paul and Thecla*. Yet fascination with suffering does not immediately make people want to suffer too, although modern times have also taught us that suicide bombers can inspire people to imitate their examples.[243] We should

[239] For this early Christian belief see Bremmer, 'Perpetua and Her Diary: Authenticity, Family and Visions', in W. Ameling (ed.), *Märtyrer und Märtyrerakten* (Stuttgart, 2002) 77-120 at 101-2 and 'Contextualizing Heaven in Third-Century North Africa', in R.S. Boustan and A.Y. Reed (eds), *Heavenly Realms and Earthly Realities in Late Antique Religions* (Cambridge, 2004) 159-73.

[240] Bremmer, 'The Motivation of Martyrs: Perpetua and the Palestinians', in B. Luchesi and K. von Stuckrad (eds), *Religion im kulturellen Diskurs. Festschrift für Hans G. Kippenberg zu seinem 65. Geburtstag / Religion in Cultural Discourse. Essays in Honor of Hans G. Kippenberg on Occasion of His 65th Birthday* (Berlin and New York, 2004) 535-54 at 549f.

[241] Harnack, *Mission und Ausbreitung*, 506f.

[242] See the important studies of J. Perkins, *The Suffering Self* (Londen and New York, 1995) and B. Shaw, 'Body/Power/Identity: Passions of the Martyrs', *J. Early Christian Studies* 4 (1996) 269-312; R. Gordon, 'The Mithraic Body: the Example of the Capua Mithraeum', in G. Casadio and P.A. Johnston (eds), *Mystic Cults in Magna Graecia* (Austin, 2009) 290-313; note also C. Spicq, *Notes de lexicographie néo-testamentaire. Supplément* (Göttingen, 1982) 658-65; Bremmer, 'Perpetua and Her Diary', 93-5.

[243] The problem is strangely underresearched, but see R.A. Pape, *Dying to Win. The Strategic Logic of Suicide Terrorism* (New York, 2005) 187-97; A. Pedahzur, *Sui-*

therefore not reject the idea out of hand, but also not exaggerate its influence. In the end, the steadfastness of martyrs, in reality or in literature, may have influenced fellow believers more than non-Christians.[244]

Stark's final chapter studies the opportunities for a new faith to appear at this particular place and time (191-203) as well as the organizational features of the Church (203-08). The first question is of course a good one, and to answer it properly one would have to study the whole of pagan religion and society at that time. For our purpose it is perhaps enough that we can speak of a 'religious market' after the first century AD, as there were several different cults competeting for adherents, although none was so exclusive as Christianity or Judaism.[245] Earlier studies often referred to the so-called Oriental religions, a term popularized by Franz Cumont (1868-1947) in his famous *Les religions orientales dans le paganism romain* (1906[1]), as important competitors with Christianity. However, in the last three decades scholars have completely abandoned the term, as it has been gradually realized that these so-called religions were just cults with a little exotic tinge in a fully developed polytheistic system.[246] This system was very hospitable to new cults, and it seems too easy to say with Stark that it was weakening as the Empire became more

cide Terrorism (Cambridge and Malden, 2005) 158-64.

[244] Thus, persuasively, Lane Fox, *Pagans and Christians*, 441; Veyne, *Quand notre monde est devenu chrétien*, 86.

[245] For the problem of the religious market-place in antiquity see J. North, 'The Development of Religious Pluralism', in J. Lieu *et al.* (eds), *The Jews Among Pagans and Christians* (London and New York, 1992) 174-93; W. Ameling, 'Pliny: The Piety of a Persecutor', in Dijkstra, *Myths, Martyrs, and Modernity*, 271-99 at 271-73.

[246] See now the new edition with an excellent introduction by C. Bonnet and F. van Haeperen: F. Cumont, *Les religions orientales dans le paganism romain* (Turin, 2006); C. Bonnet *et al.* (eds), *Religioni in contatto nel Mediterraneo antico = Mediterranea* IV (Pisa and Rome, 2008); Bonnet, *Les religions orientales dans le monde grec et romain*. For perceptive observations regarding the influence of Christianity on Cumont's ideas see W. Burkert, '"Orient" since Franz Cumont: Enrichment and Dearth of a Concept', in Bonnet, *Les religions orientales*, 105-17.

monotheistic. A growing monotheistic tendency in paganism cannot be denied,[247] but that can also be seen as a sign of its vitality.[248]

As regards the organization of early Christianity, Stark differentiates between religions that are exclusive and those that are non-exclusive. The exclusive ones are clearly stronger, and their clergy has a much closer tie with the rank and file. Roman authorities never quite understood this, since in the pre-Diocletian persecutions they often arrested the leaders but did not go after the other members of the Church, who replaced them. This attitude is well illustrated by the case of the already mentioned Peregrinus, as he could be visited in prison by fellow believers who clearly were not afraid for their own safety,[249] however strange this may seem to us today. For Stark, it is this person-to-person contact that made Christianity into such a successful movement.

Stark concludes his book with a few sketchy remarks (209-15), such as the significance of the idea of God's love and the corresponding idea of people having to love one another. This is undoubtedly an important observation but it is hardly elaborated by him. Other points briefly mentioned are the liberating social relations between the sexes and within the family, although the latter, as we have seen (§ 1), could also come with heavy costs, and a brief reflection on the ultimate factor in the Christian rise. As if it were a modern therapy, he formulates this factor as follows: 'Central doctrines of Christianity prompted and sustained attractive, liberating, and effective social relations and organizations' (211). It is

---

[247] P. Athanassiadi and M. Frede (eds), *Pagan Monotheism in Late Antiquity* (Oxford, 1999); A. Fürst, 'Christentum im Trend. Monotheistische Tendenzen in der späten Antike', *Zeitschrift für antikes Christentum* 9 (2005) 496-523 and 'Paganer und christlicher "Monotheismus"', *Jahrbuch für Antike und Christentum* 51 (2008 [2010]) 5-24; S. Mitchell and P. van Nuffelen (eds), *One God. Pagan Monotheism in the Roman Empire* (Cambridge, 2010) and *Monotheism between Pagans and Christians in Late Antiquity* (Leuven, 2010).

[248] For paganism in Late Antiquity see R. Macmullen, *Christianity and Paganism in the Fourth to Eighth Centuries* (New Haven and London, 1997); H. Leppin, 'Zum Wandel des spätantiken Heidentums', *Millennium* 1 (2004) 59-81; C. Ando, *The Matter of Gods* (Berkeley, Los Angeles, London, 2008).

[249] Bremmer, 'Peregrinus' Christian Career', in A. Hilhorst *et al.* (eds), *Flores Florentino. Dead Sea Scrolls and Other Early Jewish Studies in Honour of Florentino García Martínez* (Leiden, 2007) 729-47.

therefore not surprising that, not without the necessary exaggeration, Stark concludes: 'what Christianity gave to its converts was nothing less than their humanity' (215).

It is not that easy to pass a balanced judgement on Stark's book. It is only fair to say that when I read it for the first time ten years ago, I was impressed by its bravura style and technical expertise. However, closer inspection has shown that his treatment of subjects is often rather sketchy, his statistical exercises misguided and his knowledge of the ancient world mostly outdated. We welcome a sociologist on our turf, but a guest should also play by the rules and inform himself properly about the nature of the game. Stark, then, is not in the same league as Gibbon and Harnack. This does not mean that his insights are without value. His familiarity with the modern New Religious Movements has sensitised him to certain aspects of the rise of Christianity that ancient historians have often neglected, such as the importance of networks, the occurrence of the higher classes among early converts, Christianity's occupation of a niche in the religious market and the rationality of martyrdom. Yet a little bit more modesty regarding the value of his own insights would have served him well.

4 Concluding Observations

Although recent decades have seen serious studies of the rise of Christianity by Ramsay Macmullen, Robin Lane Fox and Paul Veyne,[250] Gibbon's shadow still looms large over the field – a sign of his towering intellect and insights, even though he wrote more than two centuries ago.[251] Every serious scholar is still in his debt, whereas the century-old collection of facts by Harnack remains the indispensable basis for any study even today. We may quarrel, and have done so, with some of their views. Yet we cannot but admire them, even though we have also noticed that they were influenced by the spirit of their own times: Gibbon by preoccupations of the Enlightenment, Harnack by those of *Kulturprotestantismus*.[252] Even Rodney Stark deserves admiration for trying to

[250] For the titles see notes 57 and 183, 39 and 44, respectively.

[251] Cf. S. Schwarz, 'Roman Historians and the Rise of Christianity: the School of Edward Gibbon', in Harris, *Spread of Christianity*, 145-60.

[252] Markschies, *Warum hat das Christentum in der Antike überlebt?*, 40 also notes

take a wholly fresh look at the problem, however unsuccessful at times and however led astray now and then by Rational Choice Theory. So what have we learned from them and what is still to be researched? Unfortunately, the ancient world has left no records of religious consumers' associations. This means that we have to make comparisons ourselves. Why was Christianity more successful than the Mithraic, Isiac or other cults? Such a quest does not offer easy answers, as the religious economy of the ancient world still poses many questions, but we will try to answer the question by looking one more time at the when, who and why of the rise of Christianity.

When did the Christians become visible in the Roman Empire, and can we distinguish certain developments in this visibility? Whereas Gibbon only made a rough start in quantifying the number of Christians, Harnack and Stark have tried to come up with more precise numbers. We have seen, though, that their computations are built on quicksand.[253] MacMullen has recently tried to improve on his predecessors by computing the space available for worshippers in churches: he thus reaches a rather low number of Christians by 300 AD.[254] Yet he does not take into account that the early Christians first met in house churches, which did not disappear overnight after Constantine. Although hard to find in archaeological excavations, their continued existence is fairly well attested in the literature; they are mentioned in imperial legislation in 383 AD, and still found in Syria even several centuries later.[255] We may grant MacMullen that we should not overestimate the number of Christians,

---

'wie viel von ganzen Forscher-Generationen zusammengetragenen Erklärungen für den Aufstieg des Christentums über eben diese Forscher verraten'.

[253] Even the often accepted computations of R. Bagnall, 'Religious Conversion and Onomastic Change in Early Byzantine Egypt', *Bulletin American Society Papyrologists* 19 (1982) 105-24, reprinted in Bagnall, *Later Roman Egypt* (Aldershot and Burlington, 2003) Ch. VIII, do not withstand proper scrutiny, cf. the bibliography of the following debate in J. Dijkstra, *Philae and the End of Ancient Egyptian Religion* (Leuven, 2008) 47 n. 1 and the criticisms of P. van Minnen, 'Hermopolis and Its Papyri', in G. Bastianini and A. Casanova (eds), *100 anni di istituzioni Fiorentine per la papirologia* (Florence, 2009) 1-15 at 5-7.

[254] MacMullen, *Second Church*, 95-114.

[255] *Codex Theodosianus* 16.5.11; Gessel, 'Organisation, Formen des Gemeindelebens', 330 (Syria); excellent and innovative, Bowes, *Private Worship, Public Values*.

but we should also not underestimate them, as he clearly does. That is as far as we can go. Instead of focussing on precise but unfounded numbers, it seems methodologically safer to point to certain trends in the rise of Christianity.

We know that the Christians were impressed by their own growth. Harnack's collection of their unanimous statements to that intent runs from Paul to Augustine.[256] In fact, there is no other ancient cult or religion with comparable self-confidence. Undoubtedly, there is exaggeration amongst these testimonies, but their consistency cannot be ignored, and certainly not refuted by adducing a single rhetorical passage from Origen, who contrasts the small number of faithful with the unbelieving Roman Empire as a whole,[257] partly because he also has many more statements to the contrary.[258] And indeed, given that Harnack can already list well over 50 congregations before the end of the first century,[259] Christianity must have spread rather quickly during and after its split from Judaism.[260] This is the more the case as, almost certainly, the number must have been rather larger than 50, given the incomplete and fragmentary nature of our tradition.[261] For this fast rise we may compare the cult of Mithras, which suddenly appears in Judaea, Raetia and Rome in the late first century AD, but is already widely present in very different

[256] Harnack, *Mission und Ausbreitung*, 529-43, further analysed by W. Kinzig, *Novitas Christiana* (Göttingen, 1994) 452-58.

[257] Origen, *Contra Celsum* 8.69, adduced by Gibbon (I.507), uncritically repeated by Lane Fox, *Pagans and Christians*, 269.

[258] Harnack, *Mission und Ausbreitung*, 535-38; B. Aland, *Frühe direkte Auseinandersetzung zwischen Christen, Heiden und Häretikern* (Berlin and New York, 2005) 5-8.

[259] Harnack, *Mission und Ausbreitung*, 621-26.

[260] For this fateful process see most recently A. Becker and A.Y. Reed (eds), *The Ways that Never Parted: Jews and Christians in Late Antiquity and the Early Middle Ages* (Tübingen, 2003); D. Boyarin, *Border Lines. The Partition of Judaeo-Christianity* (Philadelphia, 2004); Spence, *The Parting of the Ways*; J. Dunn, *The Partings of the Ways: between Christianity and Judaism and their Significance for the Character of Christianity* (London, 2006²); M. Heemstra, *The* Fiscus Judaicus *and the Parting of the Ways* (Tübingen, 2010).

[261] Thus, rightly, Hopkins, 'Christian Number', 200-03.

parts of the Roman Empire in the middle of the second century.[262] Evidently, the Roman religious system was open enough to accommodate different kinds of new cults and religions.

The feeling of impressive growth increased in the latter half of the second century and can be correlated with a feeling that the number of 'heretics' was growing too.[263] If we look at the number of congregations collected by Harnack,[264] we can see that they easily doubled until the death of Marcus Aurelius in 180 AD. This growth must have been, at least partially, responsible for the development of the monepiscopate; a more complicated organisation required a more efficient leadership. Regarding the long third century until the Council of Nicaea of 325 AD, Harnack (628-927) cannot even list the number of Christian congregations in a brief compass, but is forced to an extensive description counting many pages. It is also in this century that we witness the gradual infiltration of Christians into the imperial household as well as the equestrian and senatorial orders.[265] In the latter half of the century, the philosopher Porphyry, perhaps the sharpest pagan critic of Christianity, also noted the spread of the Christians and apparently witnessed the appearance of the first public churches in the larger cities, as he observed that the Christians were erecting 'great buildings'.[266] These, admittedly scarce, indications seem to sufficiently demonstrate that Christianity was ever spreading in the time before Constantine. Yet we have no idea about the numbers or about the precise division between town and country or between East and West, although towns were clearly much more im-

[262] M. Clauss, *The Roman Cult of Mithras*, tr. R. Gordon (New York, 2000) 21-29; R. Gordon, 'The Roman Army and the Cult of Mithras: a critical view', in Y. Le Bohec and C. Wolff (eds), *L'armée romaine et la religion* (Paris, 2009) 379-450.

[263] Justin, *I Apol.* 26.5, 58.2; Irenaeus, *Adversus haereses* 4, *Praefatio* 4; Harnack, *Mission und Ausbreitung*, 928-32; Kinzig, *Novitas Christiana*, 458 n. 68.

[264] Harnack, *Mission und Ausbreitung*, 626-28.

[265] Ph. Harland, 'Connections with Elites in the World of the Early Christians', in A.J. Blasi *et al.* (eds), *Handbook of Early Christianity: Social Science Approaches* (Walnut Creek, CA, 2002) 385-408.

[266] Spread: Porphyry, *Contra Christianos*, fr. 13 Harnack and *Vita Plotini* 16, who should have been taken into account by MacMullen, *Second Church*, 101-04. Buildings: fr. 76 Harnack.

portant in the beginning, and Christianity took much earlier root in the East than in the West.[267]

As regards the *who* of the rise, we can point to an increasing unanimity among scholars that, after the first century, Christianity no longer spread through professional missionaries but mainly via social networks.[268] Stark's comparison with modern cults is really illuminating here. Yet this new insight also raises new questions. If there were no professional missionaries, how did the steady rise take place? A first answer must probably be that there still was a certain mission consciousness among the early Christians, perhaps supported by the stories in *Acts* and the letters of Paul, which expressed itself in telling the gospel through 'local, occasional, discreetly ambiguous contacts rather than any ideologically or pragmatically coherent mission'.[269] Thus it was not only neighbours or fellow workers that spread the 'good news', but also travellers such as merchants,[270] soldiers and members of the imperial household.[271] Except for the great *metropoleis*, such as Rome, Carthage and Alexandria, ancient cities were mainly face-to-face societies, and 'abnormal' religious behaviour would have been immediately noticed and must have aroused curiosity.[272] But who were the main 'brokers' in the rise? Were they the women, whose importance in early Christianity we have often noticed?[273] Were they the adolescents and young adults who had little to lose and who may have been more important than we

[267] Harnack, *Mission und Ausbreitung*, 947-58. Interestingly, the cult of Mithras was much better represented in the Latin West, cf. Gordon, 'The Roman Army and the Cult of Mithras', 416.

[268] See most recently Reinbold, *Propaganda und Mission*, 299-341; Henderson, 'Mission and Ritual', 34-47.

[269] Henderson, 'Mission and Ritual', 46.

[270] P. Beskow, 'Mission, Trade and Emigration in the Second Century', *Svensk Exegetisk Årsbok* 35 (1970) 104-14.

[271] A.R. Birley, in Wlosok, *L'apologétique chrétienne*, 279f.

[272] Neighbours are mentioned by Justin, *I Apol.* 16.4; *Acts of Paul* 7.

[273] See also M.Y. MacDonald, 'Was Celsus Right? The Role of Women in the Expansion of Early Christianity', in D.L. Balch and C. Osiek (eds), *Early Christian Families in Context* (Grand Rapids and Cambridge, 2003) 157-84; C. Stenschke, 'Married Women and the Spread of Early Christianity', *Neotestamentica* 43 (2009) 145-94.

might think?[274] Were they the husbands whose conversions might have carried along the whole of their households? Or were all three together important, reinforcing one another? This seems to be a field where further research might still shed some light on the precise conditions of the spread.

Finally and most importantly, *why* did Christianity attract so many converts? Here we immediately run into difficulties. It is amazing how few narratives we have of individual conversions from the period under discussion. Less than a handful! And even those cannot be translated into a proper life story.[275] It cannot be stressed enough that the rise of Christianity was a creeping process that has left far fewer traces than we might have expected from such an important religious movement. Any explanation, therefore, has to be fairly general and can only be preliminary, as at the moment we cannot even differentiate conversions by class or century; the reasons to convert in the first century may well have been rather different from those in the third century. Moreover, any explanation has to take into account a number of contexts and perspectives. Let us focus here on three of them – the social, institutional and religious aspects of the rise – which may all have contributed in different ways to the conversion of different individuals.

First, there is general agreement that the lifestyle of the early Christians played an important role in the rise of Christianity. In that respect, Gibbon's ideas about the relevance of its 'pure and austere morals' have held up well, as there is plenty of evidence for the ascetic streak in early Christianity regarding meat, drink, sex and luxury.[276] Yet here too we

---

[274] Bremmer, 'Social and Religious Capital of the Early Christians', 274; add the fifteen-year old Ponticus in *Mart. Lugd.* 53 and the 21-year old Pamoun in *P.Oxy.* 70.4759.

[275] Tatian, *Or.* 29; A.D. Nock, *Conversion* (Oxford, 1933) 254-59 (Justin Martyr and Arnobius); L. Nasrallah, 'The Rhetoric of Conversion and the Construction of Experience: The Case of Justin Martyr', *Studia Patristica* 40 (Leuven, 2006) 467-74; J. Engberg, '"From among You are We. Made, not Born are Christians": Apologists' Accounts of Conversion before 310 AD', in J. Ulrich *et al.* (eds), *Continuity and Discontinuity in Early Christian Apologetics* (Frankfurt, 2009) 49-77.

[276] R. Krawiec, 'Asceticism', in Harvey and Hunter, *Oxford Handbook of Early Christian Studies*, 764-85; R. Finn, *Asceticism in the Greco-Roman World* (Cambridge, 2009); E. Baltrusch, 'Luxus II (Luxuskritik)', in *RAC* 23 (2009) 711-38.

have to be careful and should not confuse discourse with practice, as we can say hardly anything about the effects of asceticism on daily life. In modern sects, disciplining causes people to achieve.[277] Was this also a factor in the rise?

Charity must have been an important factor too. Coupled with the Christian sense of community, this social aspect must have become more important over time. We know that Roman criminal law became harsher in Late Antiquity and that the economy deteriorated. Both factors will have made it more attractive for people to join a Christian congregation.[278] Finally, we have noticed the bridging and bonding that must have been promoted by a certain egalitarian ethos, which was also expressed by the usage of terms derived from the Athenian democracy (§ 1), although the ethos became less egalitarian when more people joined the Church.[279]

Another important factor must have been Gibbon's fifth cause: the government of the Church. We cannot stress enough that the way the Church was governed was totally unique in antiquity, as there was nothing comparable in Greco-Roman religion. The many contacts between individual churches via letters in the first two centuries as well as the later provincial and national councils and synods must have created and sustained a feeling of unity within the heterogeneous Roman Empire.[280] To Celsus, the notion of a global ethic and a single pattern of worship seemed utopian and wholly unrealistic,[281] but that is what all the translocal contacts did achieve, despite local variations. The unity will also have helped Christians to identify with their community and thus to better equip them for difficult times such as persecutions.[282]

---

[277] Stark and Finke, *Acts of Faith*, 204.

[278] M. Atkins and R. Osborne (eds), *Poverty in the Roman World* (Cambridge, 2006); A. Bowman and A. Wilson (eds), *Quantifying the Roman Economy: methods and problems* (Oxford, 2009).

[279] Stark and Finke, *Acts of Faith*, 205.

[280] E. Ferguson, 'Creeds, Councils, and Canons', in Harvey and Hunter, *Oxford Handbook of Early Christian Studies*, 427-45 at 434-38.

[281] Origen, *Contra Celsum*, 8.72.

[282] Harnack, *Mission und Ausbreitung*, 259-89; Kinzig, *Novitas Christiana*, 145-71. For letters, bishops and ecclesiastical meetings see also D. Mendels, *The Media Revolution of Early Christianity* (Grand Rapids and Cambridge, 1999) 151-77;

The frequent contact and feeling of unity must have been realised rather early. Otherwise, for example, it would be difficult to explain the fact that early Christianity unanimously chose the codex instead of the Jewish scroll as *the* medium for its Sacred Scripture (§ 2). But what was the relation between unity and diversity in early Christianity? Since Walter Bauer's famous book on heresy and orthodoxy in early Christianity,[283] there is an ongoing dispute concerning the measure of orthodoxy of the early Church. In our postmodern age it is of course fashionable to speak of 'Christianities' instead of Christianity, and there is no doubt that there were many local and regional differences in the Roman Empire that must have influenced local manifestations of Christianity. Yet if we stress diversity too much, it will be difficult to explain the rise of the 'orthodox' Church, which Celsus already pictured as the 'Great Church' in the later second century.[284] Looking at Rome, the only city for which we have sufficient early data, we can see that in the middle of the second century there still was an impressive theological pluralism in addition to the 'orthodox' congregations: Marcionites, Carpocratians, Valentinians,[285] Quartodecumans and so on, who, except for the Marcionites, were still seen as fellow Christians.[286] Yet at the end of that century the 'orthodox' Church was prevailing, the others condemned as 'heretics', and the Biblical canon established in its main lines.[287] How

M.-F. Baslez, *Comment notre monde est devenu chrétien* (Paris, 2008) 120-26.

[283] W. Bauer, *Rechtgläubigkeit und Ketzerei im ältesten Christentum* (Tübingen 1934[1], 1964[2]), = *Orthodoxy and Heresy in Earliest Christianity*, ed. and suppl. by R.A. Kraft and G. Kroedel with a team from the Philadelphia Seminar on Christian Origins (Philadelphia, 1971), cf. the excellent discussion by C. Markschies, *Kaiserzeitliche christliche Theologie und ihre Institutionen* (Tübingen, 2007) 337-83.

[284] Origen, *Contra Celsum* 5.59 and 5.61.

[285] E. Thomassen, *The Spiritual Seed: the Church of the "Valentinians"* (Leiden, 2006).

[286] But see Lampe, *From Paul to Valentinus*, 381-412; E. Thomassen, 'Orthodoxy and Heresy in Second-Century Rome', *Harvard Theological Review* 97 (2004) 241-56.

[287] The study of the growth of the canon is a small industry. See most recently, with extensive bibliographies, K. Greschat, 'Die Entstehung des neutestamentlichen Kanons: Fragestellungen und Themen der neueren Forschung', *Verkündigung und Forschung* 51 (2006) 56-63 and Markschies, *Kaiserzeitliche christliche Theologie*,

this did happen and why 'orthodoxy' prevailed over pluralism is still obscure,[288] and it does not help that good information about the later second century is scarce.[289] Here there is still plenty of work to be done.

The last and perhaps most difficult to define factor is the religious one. Evidence is scarce, but Gibbon and Harnack had no doubts about the religious factor. The former thought of the immortality of the soul and the performance of miracles, neither of which has proved to be persuasive (§ 1), whereas the latter came up with a whole series of statements that were hardly supported by any evidence (§ 2). On the other hand, it is typical of our secularised times that modern studies about the rise of Christianity, with the notable exception of Veyne,[290] have had relatively little to say about its religious attractions. Yet I would like to single out two important aspects.

First, as inscriptions and votive reliefs show, in Greco-Roman religion, especially in the East, the distance between deity and worshipper was steadily increasing.[291] For the early Christians, in contrast, the love of God must have been especially important. Any reader of the New Testament will be immediately struck by expressions, such as that God is 'the Father' and the Christians his 'children'. He loves his children and has chosen them. To quote an important study of this phenomenon: 'the common language of the Leaders, which in these particulars is probably shared generally by the members, represents God as participating per-

215-335; see also P.S. Alexander and J.-D. Kaestli (eds), *The Canon of Scripture in Jewish and Christian Tradition* (Lausanne, 2007); E. Thomassen (ed.), *Canon and Canonicity* (Copenhagen, 2010).

[288] Av. Cameron, 'The Violence of Orthodoxy', in E. Iricinschi and H. Zellentin (eds), *Heresy and Identity in Late Antiquity* (Tübingen, 2008) 102-14 well stresses the need for more research into 'orthodoxy' instead of the presently more popular 'heresy'.

[289] W.A. Löhr, 'Das antike Christentum im zweiten Jahrhundert. Neue Perspektiven seiner Erforschung', *Theologische Literaturzeitung* 127 (2002) 247-62.

[290] Veyne, *Quand notre monde est devenu chrétien*, 35-65.

[291] Inscriptions: H.S. Versnel, 'Religious Mentality in Ancient Prayer' and H.W. Pleket, 'Religious History as the History of Mentality: 'The Believer' as Servant of the Deity in the Greek World', in H.S. Versnel (ed.), *Faith, Hope and Worship* (Leiden, 1981) 1-64 and 152-92, respectively. Votive reliefs: G. Schörner, *Votive im römischen Griechenland* (Stuttgart, 2003) 187-98 (with thanks to Anja Klöckner).

sonally in the direct, feeling-charged community of the house churches'.[292] One can easily see that this close connection with God or Christ, sometimes not easily distinguished, helped the early Christians through their hardships, as many *Acts* of the Christian martyrs eloquently attest.[293] The already mentioned *Passion of Perpetua* (§ 2) provides a moving example. In a vision shortly before her execution, she saw herself ascending to heaven where God/Christ awaited her and greeted her with the words 'Welcome, child' (*Passio Perpetuae* 4.9). In fact, it is striking that so many martyrs confessed their faith with the words: 'I am a Christian' (*Christianus/a sum*), which probably popularised the name 'Christians' as followers of Christ, whereas in the first two centuries other names had been current as well.[294] There is nothing comparable in Greco-Roman religion to this close tie between believer and divinity.[295]

A second religious factor must have been the belief in salvation and condemnation. Paul and his associates firmly believed in the resurrection and held this belief out as a consolation to the Thessalonian Christians (*1 Thess.* 4.13-8). The same belief, but perhaps more literally understood, is very apparent in the *Acts* of the martyrs, who happily underwent their execution in firm belief of their immediate salvation. In the case of the Spanish bishop Fructuosus, this belief was so intense that his parishioners saw the bishop, still bound to the stake, go straight to heaven after having been burned alive (*Passio Fructuosi* 5). And just as early Christians believed in instant salvation, so they firmly believed in their opponents going straight to hell. When the Roman governor told the aged Smyrnean bishop Polycarp: 'Since you are not afraid of the animals, then I shall have you consumed by fire – unless you change your mind'. He answered: 'The fire you threaten me with burns merely for a

---

[292] W. Meeks, *The First Urban Christians* (New Haven and London, 1983) 170.

[293] Bremmer, *Rise and Fall*, 103f.

[294] Bremmer, *Rise and Fall*, 105-8; add *Acta Abitiniarum* 5, 7, 10 and 13-18; P. Canart and R. Pintaudi, 'Il martirio di san Pansofio', *Analecta Papyrologica* 16-17 (2004-05) 189-245 at 197 (*c.* 3); see also T. Hegedus, 'Naming Christians in Antiquity', *Studies in Religion* 32 (2004) 173-90; D.G. Horrell, 'The Label *Christianoi*: 1 Pet 4.16 and the Formation of Christian Identity', *J. Bibl. Lit.* 126 (2007) 361-81, all to be added to Luijendijk, *Greetings in the Lord*, 38-40.

[295] In general see now L.W. Hurtado, *Lord Jesus Christ: Devotion to Jesus in earliest Christianity* (Grand Rapids, 2003).

time and is soon extinguished. It is clear you are ignorant of the fire of the everlasting punishment and of the judgement that is to come, which awaits the impious. Why then do you hesitate? Come, do what you will' (*Martyrium Polycarpi* 11.2). And when the aforementioned Perpetua was led into the arena and came into sight of the governor who was responsible for her execution, she and her fellow martyrs told him: 'You condemned us, but God you!' (*Passio Perpetuae* 18.8).[296]

It is time to come to a close. In its unity, exclusivity, social practices and religious beliefs Christianity offered a combination that was both unique and clearly highly attractive to the inhabitants of the Roman Empire,[297] even though explanations of individual choices are hard to find. Yet we need not believe in a necessary victory of Christianity. What would have happened without Constantine is anybody's guess, and the eventual victory of Islam in the East suggests that the new faith was more vulnerable than its early martyrs may have thought. Yet without those converts of the first three centuries, Christianity would never have become the most influential world religion of our history. As we are gathered here in the aula, we will have different opinions about that victory. Some of you are believers, others doubters and perhaps most of you non-believers. But we are all, to a certain extent, cultural Christians who are indebted to the Christian heritage. That heritage deserves to be preserved and studied today. And the best institution in which to do that is the Groningen Faculty of Theology and Religious Studies.

---

[296] These passages have been overlooked by Veyne, *Quand notre monde est devenu chrétien*, 52-55.

[297] J.B. Rives, 'Christian Expansion and Christian Ideology', in Harris, *Spread of Christianity*, 15-41 well stresses the exclusivity, homogeneity and 'totalization' of early Christianity and concludes at 41: 'Yet in the end we must acknowledge that Christianity represented something genuinely novel, if not absolutely *sui generis*'; Veyne, *Quand notre monde est devenu chrétien*, 48-9, 59, also comments on the fact that new religions sometimes offer something completely new and should not always be explained from the *Zeitgeist* and K. Dowden, 'Rationales for the Adoption of Christianity', in Dijkstra, *Myths, Martyrs, and Modernity*, 409-24, even speaks of a 'new paradigm'.

Epilogue

At the time of writing this epilogue, December 2009, it is exactly twenty years ago since I took the train to Groningen to be interviewed by the committee that had to advise about the succession of Hans Kippenberg, my predecessor in the Groningen Chair of Religious Studies. The interview went well, and in the evening the chairman of the committee, the late Adam van der Woude (1927-2000), phoned to tell me that I would be recommended for the position. Twenty years later, I would like briefly to thank here those persons who, along the way, have been especially important to me in my academic career.

Looking back, it is appropriate that I first thank my father and mother, who instilled in me a love for history, but who also displayed an ethos of work and concern for others that I have always found admirable.

My own interest in ancient religion, my main research speciality, developed especially during my military service (1970-1972), when I had plenty of time to read. At the time it was above all the work of the Dutch Latinist and historian of religion Hendrik Wagenvoort (1886-1976) that caught my attention and made me decide to concentrate on Greek religion. Here it was in particular Walter Burkert's focus on myth and ritual that fascinated me, a fascination that has remained with me to the present day. All these years his work has been a constant source of inspiration, and my own studies have frequently been 'eine Art Gespräch mit Vorschlägen von mir', as Burkert rightly wrote to me after my latest book.

It was with Burkert and a number of younger friends and scholars – Richard Buxton, Claude Calame, Fritz Graf, Albert Henrichs, Robert Parker and the late Christiane Sourvinou-Inwood (1945-2007) – that I brought out a collection on Greek mythology in 1987 that still represents a good illustration of the insights of that time.[298] I consider it a privilege that I have been able to stay in contact with and learn from all of them, even though we have our different interests and approaches. I would also like to mention here Christoph Auffarth, Ken Dowden, Bob

[298] J.N. Bremmer (ed.), *Interpretations of Greek Mythology* (London and Sydney, 1987). Most of us were still at the beginning of our university career and, as Cristiano Grottanelli, *History of Religions* 29 (1989) 58-64 at 58 noted in an excellent review, only 'in their early forties'.

Fowler and Einar Thomassen, who have equally proved to be sources of friendship and inspiration over the years.

I have worked much less on Roman myth and religion. But whenever I do, I know that I have an excellent critic in the person of Nicholas Horsfall. It was a delight to work together on our book on Roman myth and mythography,[299] and it is one of the boons of the internet that friendships can be maintained even with those that live *in ultima Scotia*.

Around 1980, when I was still in Utrecht, Jan den Boeft proposed that we should give lectures together on the *Acta martyrum*, the reports of the executions of ancient Christian martyrs. His proposal introduced me to the world of early Christianity, which has been part of my research ever since. The interest in martyrs and early Christianity I also share with my colleague Ton Hilhorst. Over the years Ton saved me from numerous mistakes, but he also let me always profit generously from his impressive erudition. Although we may not quite attain the goal of old-fashioned *Altertumswissenschaft*, we certainly share the ideal.

My stay in Groningen introduced me to the world of the Dead Sea Scrolls as studied and edited in our Qumran Institute. Their profound knowledge of the world of Second Temple Judaism has always made it a great pleasure to talk to and to work with its successive directors: Adam van der Woude, Florentino García Martínez, Eibert Tigchelaar and Mladen Popović.

In Groningen, the research group Religious Symbols constitutes the forum where local students of ancient religion, anthropology, church history and architecture, Egyptology, history, Indian Studies and Islamic Studies meet and discuss the latest developments in their fields. I have always taken much pleasure in these interdisciplinary discussions. In the last two decades the kernel of the group has been, together with me, my closest colleagues: Hans Bakker, Lourens van den Bosch and Yme Kuiper. From Hans I learned everything I know about the fascinating world of ancient and modern India, the importance of which he so passionately impresses upon me and my colleagues; with Lourens I shared the interest in the history of our subject and the world of liberal Christianity, and with Yme I discussed current affairs, anthropology of religion and the more recent history of the Netherlands over many lunches. Our

[299] J.N. Bremmer and N.M. Horsfall, *Roman Myth and Mythography* (London, 1987).

dialogues at the time of his inaugural and now my farewell lecture are two highlights of our fertile cooperation.

The internet not only enables communication with friends near and far away but also betrays things that should be secret. Looking recently at some of my publications on Amazon, I noticed that my colleagues had prepared a *Festschrift* for me.[300] It may be unusual to do so, but I will not forego the chance here to thank the editors: Jitse Dijkstra, Justin Kroesen and Yme Kuiper. Jitse and Justin represent the best of the younger generation of our Faculty: ambitious, erudite but also collegial and interested in the work of others. As with Yme, each in their own way has been a pleasure to work and to be with, and I am sure that this will remain the case in the future.

Finally, none of this would have been possible without the continuing support of Christine in good and bad times. She was always there for me and has made my career possible. I dedicate this lecture to her and hope that, together with our children and grandchildren, we may still enjoy each other's companionship for many years to come.[301]

---

[300] See my bibliography.

[301] Richard Buxton, old friend and colleague, kindly corrected the English of the Epilogue.

Bibliography of Jan N. Bremmer

There is a complete bibliography of my writings in J. Dijkstra, J. Kroesen and Y. Kuiper (eds), *Myths, Martyrs, and Modernity: Studies in the History of Religions in Honour of Jan N. Bremmer* (Leiden: Brill, 2010) xxxix-lvi. I therefore list here only the most recent publications:

Forthcoming

(co-editor, with Marco Formisano) *Perpetua's Passions* (Oxford: Oxford University Press)

'Felicitas: the Martyrdom of a Young African Woman', *ibidem*, ms of 18 pp.

'Divinities in the Orphic Gold Leaves', in F. Graf (ed.), *The Orphic Gold Leaves. A Conference*, Leiden: Brill, ms of 26 pp.

'*Manteis*, Magic, Mysteries and Mythography: Messy Margins of Polis Religion?', *Kernos* 23 (2010), ms of 23 pp.

'A Brief History of the Study of Greek Mythology', in K. Dowden and N. Livingstone (eds), *Blackwell Companion to Greek Mythology*, Oxford: Blackwell, ms of 22 pp.

'The Eleusinian Mysteries: A 'Thin' Description', in *Mystery and Secrecy in Honor of ...*, ms of 18 pp.

'Orphic, Roman, Jewish and Christian Tours of Hell: Observations on the *Apocalypse of Peter*', in E. Eynikel, F. García Martínez, T. Nicklas and J. Verheyden (eds), *Other Worlds and their Relation to this World = Journal for the Study of Judaism*, Supplements, Leiden: Brill, ms of 16 pp.

(with Jan den Boeft) 'Notiunculae Martyrologicae VI: *Passio Perpetuae* 2, 16 and 17', in *Persecution and Martyrdom in Late Antiquity (100-700) AD. Essays in Honour of ...*, ms of 16 pp.

'Human Sacrifice in Euripides' Iphigeneia in Tauris: Greek and Barbarian', in P. Bonnechere and R. Gagné (eds), *Representations of Human Sacrifice*, Liège: CIERGA, ms of 15 pp.

'Jews and Spartans: Abrahamic cousins?', in M. Goodman, G. van Kooten and J. van Ruiten (eds), *Abraham, the Nations, and the Hagarites*, Leiden: Brill, ms of 14 pp.

'Michael Jameson and the Study of Greek Religion', in M. Jameson, *Cults and Rites in Ancient Greece*, Cambridge: Cambridge University Press, ms of 9 pp.

2010

The Rise of Christianity through the Eyes of Gibbon, Harnack and Rodney Stark, Groningen: Faculteit Godgeleerdheid en Godsdienstwetenschap; second edition: Groningen: Barkhuis Publishing & Groningen University Library

(editor), *The Pseudo-Clementines*, Leuven: Peeters

'Pseudo-Clementines: Texts, Dates, Places, Authors and Magic', *ibidem*, 1-23

'Apion and Anoubion in the *Homilies*', *ibidem*, 73-92

(co-editor, with Andrew Erskine), *The Gods of Ancient Greece: Identities and Transformations*, Edinburgh: Edinburgh University Press

'The Greek Gods in the Twentieth Century', *ibidem*, 1-18

'Hephaistos Sweats or How to Construct an Ambivalent God', *ibidem*, 193-208

'From Holy Books to Holy Bible: an Itinerary from Ancient Greece to Modern Islam via Second Temple Judaism and Early Christianity', in M. Popović (ed.), *Authoritative Scriptures in Ancient Judaism*, Leiden: Brill, 327-60

'Walter Burkert on Ancient Myth and Ritual: Some Personal Observations', in A. Bierl and W. Braungart (eds), *Gewalt und Opfer. Im Dialog mit Walter Burkert*, Berlin and New York: De Gruyter, 71-86

'Human Sacrifice in Ancient Societies', in Royal Opera House, London, programme for the new production of Verdi's *Aida*, 29-33

2009

'Die Karriere der Seele: Vom antiken Griechenland ins moderne Europa', in H. Kippenberg *et al.* (eds), *Handbuch Europäische Religionsgeschichte*, 2 vols, Göttingen: Vandenhoeck & Ruprecht, 2.497-524

'Christian Hell: From the *Apocalypse of Peter* to the *Apocalypse of Paul*', *Numen* 56, 298-325

'The Golden Bough: Orphic, Eleusinian and Hellenistic-Jewish Sources of Virgil's Underworld in *Aeneid* VI', *Kernos* 22, 183-208

'Zeus' Own Country: Cult and Myth in *The Pride of Halicarnassus*', in U. Dill and C. Walde (eds), *Antike Mythen. Medien, Transformationen und Konstruktionen*, Berlin and New York: De Gruyter, 292-312

'Eric Cossee: predikant te Rotterdam, professor in Groningen', in M. de Baar and M. van Dijk (eds), *Herinnering en identiteit in het Vrijzinnig Protestantisme*, Hilversum: Verloren, 173-87

'Myth, Mythology and Mythography', in G. Boys-Stones *et al.* (eds), *Oxford Handbook of Hellenic Studies*, Oxford: Oxford University Press, 678-86

'Ian Buruma: an intellectual cosmopolitan', *Praemium Erasmianum Yearbook* 2008, 21-27

'Afterlife: IV: Greco-Roman Antiquity', in H.-J. Klauck *et al.* (eds), *Encyclopedia of the Bible and its Reception*, Berlin and New York: de Gruyter, 1.541-45.

'Philogelos', in *Kindlers Literatur Lexikon*, third edition, Tübingen: Metzler, 12.775

Index of names, subjects and passages

About the author

Jan Bremmer was born in 1944 in Groningen in the North of the Netherlands. He studied Classics and Spanish at the Free University, Amsterdam (1962-19790). From 1970-1972 he was in the Dutch Military Intelligence. In 1974 he became Assistant/Associate Professor Ancient History at the University of Utrecht. In 1979 he received his PhD from the Free University with his dissertation *The Early Greek Conception of the Soul*, which was published in 1983 by the Princeton University Press and has stayed in print ever since. In 1990 he was appointed to the Chair of Religious Studies at the Faculty of Theology and Religious Studies of the University of Groningen. He has widely published on Greek, Roman, early Christian and contemporary religion, social history, and the historiography of ancient religion. He has been a Fellow of the Center for Hellenic Studies in Washington (1980-1981), a Member of the Institute of Advanced Study in Princeton (2000), a Canterbury Fellow of the University of Christchurch (New Zealand: 2002), the Inaugural Getty Villa Professor at the Getty Research Institute (Los Angeles: 2006-2007) and Visiting Leventis Professor at the University of Edinburgh (2007). In the spring of 2006 his contributions to scholarship and university life were nationally recognised when the Queen appointed him Officer in the Order of Orange-Nassau. He retired on 1 December 2009.